To: John

Merry Chris...

and great Millenium —

Dec. 1999
("Nothing But Net")

Van Chancellor

"Go Comets"

Nothin' But
A Champion

The Story of Van Chancellor
Three-time WNBA Coach of the Year

Tom A. Savage

I want to thank David Stern, Val Ackerman, and the twenty-nine NBA owners who took a chance and started a women's basketball league known as the WNBA. I want especially to thank one of those owners, Les Alexander, for taking a chance on a country boy from Mississippi and hiring me—it's been the thrill of a lifetime.

For my wife, Betty, and my children, Johnny and Renee.

—Van Chancellor

For my wife, Nancy—

Thank you for putting up with me as I work in this crazy business.

—Tom Savage

ACKNOWLEDGMENTS

Van Chancellor and Tom Savage would like to thank the following for their assistance in creating Nothin' But a Champion:

A special thanks to
The Demontrond Automotive Group
and the entire DeMontrond Family.

Houston Cellular

Krispy Kreme Doughnuts

Bob Roten - Urbana Restaurant & Bar, Inc.

Harman Sports, Inc.

Steve Conner @ The Lucid Edge

Peter Burwash International

Houston's WB39

CONTENTS

Introduction

I REALIZE I'VE ONLY WORKED in the sports communications industry since 1991, but I can honestly say that I've never met a more down-to-earth, homespun and gracious coach than Van Chancellor.

From what I've seen in my travels over the past nine years, I've realized that each coach has a different way of handling different situations. Coaching is a unique profession, and each coach I've worked with is different in how he or she handles stress, the media, and the pressures of winning. Van faces each of them with a smile on his face and a chuckle behind his deep southern drawl. The ups and downs he's faced, not only over the last three years as head coach of the Comets but during his entire thirty-four-year coaching career, are incredible. But after each success and each pitfall, he seems to respond in the same manner—always moving ahead.

There isn't an ounce of arrogance in Van Chancellor's behavior. I've been with him on many occasions; whether it be dinner, a league function or just watching a game, and I can't remember a time when he didn't go out of his way to shake hands and talk with as many people as possible. He wants to be everyone's friend, and it's hard to find someone who doesn't want to return the favor.

My first encounter with him came on April 24, 1997 during the inaugural WNBA draft. It was Van's first day on the job and it was the first time I would ever have the chance to talk with him. He arrived early at the team's front offices, and, for a fifty-four-year-old man, he was as anxious and inspired as anyone I've ever known. By luck of the draw, the Comets received the first pick overall in the draft and Van was ready to make history that morning with the first selection.

With the number one pick, Van had a hard time choosing between Tina Thompson and another veteran player he originally had his heart set on. He had a handful of people in the room helping him with the draft and they were split between Tina and the veteran player. The veteran player had a storied past: she had led her team to multiple college championships and also had an Olympic Gold medal in her possession. No one in the room had ever seen Tina play except during televised games. Watching Van trying to make this decision was my first experience in watching this charismatic coach do his thing. His way of doing things is something I got used to and as the first season went on, it's something I enjoyed being around.

As time drew closer for the start of the draft, Van went around the table and asked everybody, one last time, whom they thought his new WNBA team should select. It went back and forth between the two players the entire way around the room and it seemed Van was no closer to a decision than he'd been hours earlier.

Then, out of nowhere, Van looked down at me and said, "What do you think, boy? Do you have an opinion on who we should take?" That in itself floored me. I was amazed first off that he was actually asking all these other people for their opinions—the last thing I expected was for him to ask for my thoughts. Although the best I could muster was, "Uh, no . . . I'm just here to take down the information," it comforted me, and I think Van and I began our friendship from that point on.

"I like you, son," he said to me later after the draft was

over. "When I start a new job I want things done a certain way. I want my own people. I like things done the Lady Rebel way. I think you fit that mold."

The Lady Rebel way was his reference to the way things were done at Ole Miss, where he'd spent the previous nineteen years as the women's head coach. I'd never been to Ole Miss, and still never have, but I could tell from that day on that this was going to work; that this would be a good relationship.

I've seen coaches get choked up over wins and losses and I've seen them give and receive compliments, but I've never seen a coach do both with such sincerity.

Chapter 1
An Unforgettable Day

"WE AIN'T SETTLIN' FOR NOTHIN' but a championship!" Those were the words Van Chancellor used moments before his team took the floor in Houston to face the New York Liberty for the inaugural WNBA Championship game on August 30, 1997. There was incredible excitement in his voice as his team huddled for the final time in the locker room. He had a grin on his face, and the confident words of settling for nothing but a championship poured out of his mouth in his typically deep southern drawl.

Van's been a coach since 1965; he clearly remembers the days of coaching in front of twenty people in many small high school gymnasiums in tiny towns throughout his home state of Mississippi. Now he coaches in front of sellout crowds all over the country and the scene puts a grin on his face every time. While a head coach at the University of Mississippi for nineteen years, he'd seen the sport of women's basketball get bigger and bigger but never would have guessed it was going to reach the magnitude that it did at the inaugural championship game. As he took the floor just moments before tip-off, walking through the tunnel that connected the locker room to the playing court, the roar of the crowd hit him and he was overcome with numerous thoughts of his years in coaching leading up to that moment.

Van knew the game was a sellout at Compaq Center, just like it was for the season opener against Phoenix earlier in the year, but that championship game against New York will stick with him forever. Van is the definition of a good ol' country boy from Mississippi, but he's definitely seen his share of major sporting events, and says that he's never heard anything as loud as the Compaq Center was on August 30, 1997.

It was easily the biggest game of his career and he had a hunger to win that game more than any in his previous thirty-two years as a head coach. Van tends to get a little nervous ('little' being the operative word) before games and there's no question that this championship game had his attention. He was definitely nervous, but he didn't let anyone see it—especially his players. They had enough on their minds; the last thing they needed was to see him walking around wringing his hands and pacing the locker room floor. Every player on the Comets roster had her hands full with the Liberty, and Van wanted to do all he could not to add to the pressure that already surrounded the day.

For the Comets to even be in the inaugural championship game was a mild surprise; to be hosting the game was nothing short of a miracle. Throughout the entire season, there weren't many in WNBA circles who thought the Comets had a shot at being the number one seed throughout the playoffs. Houston trailed New York, its main rival in the Eastern Conference, by three and a-half games with just three weeks remaining in the regular season, and the thought of catching the Liberty seemed out of reach. New York got off to such a quick start at the beginning of the season and went 7-0, including three wins against Houston. Their lead down the stretch should have been insurmountable but Houston dug in and was able to come back and win the division. Van has said that the fact that Houston caught New York and secured the number one seed amazed him more than anything else about the first year. Clearly it was a sign of things to come from this Houston team that has shown a lot of heart over the last three seasons.

When the Comets trailed New York by three and a half games with just three weeks remaining in the regular season, the team was in Los Angeles for a game against the Sparks. Houston defeated the Sparks 81-57 to improve to 11-6 on the season. It was a huge road win at the midway point in the season. A day before the game, the Comets practiced at Southwest Junior College in Los Angeles, and Van pulled me aside before practice started.

At Southwest Junior College, there are three courts in the basketball facility, and Van took me to one of the courts at the end of the building. I walked with him around the court, many times. It's something he does while the team is getting taped, stretching and getting ready for practice. He walks and walks and walks a little more until he's worn a path around the outside the court. He was visibly upset as we walked and talked. His team was 10-6 at the time and hadn't been playing very well. One of his starters was late for practice and I could sense that this was going to be one of those long days in the middle of the season. I knew my bus ride back to the hotel was going to be delayed because this had all the earmarks of a long, bad and boring couple of hours. I tried to ease his frustrations and get him thinking about a possible run at the playoffs.

"Does this team have enough to win this thing this year?" I asked him.

"Are you crazy?" Van said as he stopped walking and looked at me. I knew it must have been a bad question because I finally got him to stop walking for a second. But we resumed walking with Van shaking his head.

"Have you been watching practice lately? This team doesn't have nearly enough horses to win it all," he said.

But his mood changed just twenty-four hours later with the big win at the Great Western Forum. The win over the Sparks really seemed to turn things around for the Comets in the first season. There were eleven games remaining on the schedule and Houston went 7-2 over the next nine games to catch and pass New York for the conference championship. In a short two-week span, Van's Comets went from fighting for a playoff spot to being the number one seed and hosting two playoff games—or at the very least one playoff game. Just like every other basketball coach on the planet, Van hates looking past an opponent, and he knew the Charlotte Sting would be ready for their semifinal game on August 28.

Fortunately, Houston was able to get past Charlotte, but not without a price. The Comets' starting center, Wanda Guyton, suffered a nasty blow to the head midway through the second half when she collided with teammate Tina Thompson as the two were fighting for a rebound. Wanda quickly lost consciousness and it was one of the scariest things I've ever witnessed. She left on a stretcher and was rushed to Methodist Hospital in Houston. She was drifting in and out of consciousness when they lifted her into the awaiting ambulance. She opened her eyes occasionally and looked at Van and those attending to her but I could tell from the look in her glassed-over eyes that she didn't have any idea who any of us were. That hit against the hardwood of the Compaq Center floor was a bell-ringer.

The Guyton incident happened on Thursday and the championship game against New York was Saturday. Van was really hoping Wanda could recover from the shot to her head because without her he didn't think his team stood a chance against New York. The Liberty were so much more physical and bigger than Houston, and Van feared they would eventually wear his team down. During the regular season, Wanda missed three games because of a nagging back injury, and the Comets went 1-2 without her in the lineup. The thought of losing her for the championship game crushed him, and he knew he needed her healthy and ready to play on Saturday.

Even though everyone in the building at shoot-around the morning of the championship game was convinced Wanda wouldn't play, Van still thought he had a shot at getting her healthy. It was wishful thinking more than anything else. Everybody saw her having trouble sitting up straight in a chair or even completing sentences, but Van seemed blind to it all. I must have asked him ten times how I should list Wanda in our pre-game notes package that we provide the media. Each time I got a disgusted "probable" from Van. I'm sure I drove him crazy with that question the morning of the championship game, but every time I asked I was waiting for him to finally concede that she wasn't going to play. I'm not a coach and I'm not a doctor, but anybody in the place could tell Wanda Guyton wasn't going to put on a uniform in a few short hours and play basketball. I would have taken 10-to-1 odds she wouldn't have known her own name.

We officially listed Wanda as "probable;" as game time approached, Van still hadn't given up on his game plan of having her play. Not only did he have her playing in his mind, but when I talked with him a few hours before the game he had her starting! Every scenario he talked to me about had Wanda in the play, and it was obvious he didn't want to face the reality that she wasn't going to be on the floor. But as tip-off grew closer, our team doctors and trainers informed Van that there was no way she could play. Van has said that he thinks back on it now and it was so obvious—he just didn't want to see it.

There were a lot of ups and downs during the inaugural season, but being notified that Wanda wouldn't play upset Van more than anything else. He secluded himself in a small dressing room and it was all he could do to keep from crying. His emotions ran wild over the next fifteen minutes because he was convinced that without her playing his chances of leading the Comets to the first WNBA championship diminished dramatically. He took the job in April, and those fifteen minutes sitting in his small locker room were the most depressing time since taking the job.

It was a tough break, but Van knew he had to spin it to his team and come up with something good. He was running out of time for pre-game talks and preparations, and he knew the team would miss Wanda's ability on the court. He had to break the bad news to his team and had to put a positive spin on it. Van puts a lot of thought into his pre-game speeches and I've heard my share of his talks. From a John Wayne gunfight to David and Goliath, Van had a bunch of them, and he bounced them off me, our play-by-play announcer Jim Kozimor, or his assistant coaches.

One of Van's least favorite things about coaching basketball is the pre-game time. He obviously gets nervous before games, but mostly he simply runs out of things to do. Coaching women's basketball, there's obviously going to be a significant amount of time that he can't be in the locker room before game time. I'm sure Peggie Gillom, Van's assistant coach for twenty years before accepting the Texas A&M head coaching position in 1998, has heard every story Van's ever told. She deserves an award because he's got a vast library of stories.

Before games, Van would talk to her, his other assistant coaches Kevin Cook or Alisa Scott, the radio broadcasters, TV personalities, newspaper beat writers, the guy selling popcorn, or just about anyone who would listen. If he can't find anyone, he naps.

But after receiving the news about Wanda, he didn't want to be around anyone and the thought of a nap was clearly out of the question. He began to feel sorry for himself because he'd come so far, and to have this news delivered to him just forty-five minutes before tip-off was

WNBA." At that point he was done feeling sorry for himself and he knew that he had to concentrate on what players he did have available.

An incredible motivator, Van was on top of his game for the inaugural championship. From the time I met him on the WNBA's first draft day, all the way through three WNBA championship seasons, Van was looking to inspire and motivate. On the day of the first WNBA championship game, his inspiration and motivation were key in leading the Comets to the championship.

Wanda was gone, but Van knew there had to be a solution—or at least an alternate game plan that he could deliver to his team. He'd been putting together game plans for more than thirty years and knew somehow that he could put something together to compensate for Wanda's absence. I was with him when he sat and talked with his coaches before his pregame speech. Assistant coach Kevin Cook said something that jogged Van's memory and you could start to see the Mississippi wheels turning.

Van began to remember what Kevin said to him earlier in the day at shoot-around about Houston's backup center, Tammy Jackson, and her impressive play the last time that Houston met the Liberty. Kevin had talked to Van several times about it earlier in the day, but at that point in Van's mind, Wanda was still going to play and he wouldn't need to lean on Jackson. But as they began to talk, you could see Van coming around and remembering what Kevin had said about Houston's 70-55 win at Madison Square Garden late in the season. It was Houston's only victory over New York during the regular season, and Guyton played just thirteen minutes while Jackson saw the bulk of the minutes in the post.

She played thirty-one minutes in that game—far and away her season-high and also clearly her best game of the season. She grabbed a game high twelve rebounds and, more

She played thirty-one minutes in that game—far and away her season-high and also clearly her best game of the season. She grabbed a game high twelve rebounds and, more importantly, shut down New York's Kym Hampton, who Van feared in the middle because of her solid post play. Van also remembered talking with Tammy a few days earlier; she'd commented on how she thought she matched up well against Hampton. All of the information began to sink in when the three talked. Earlier in the day, Van didn't give it much thought but I knew he had heard it. He just hadn't wanted to listen because he wanted Wanda on the floor so badly.

With a renewed spirit and the inspirational wheels churning, Van headed back to the Comets' locker room to tell his team about the pending situation. The author of many self-awarded Pulitzer Prize winning pre-game speeches, Van didn't have much time to put together a tearjerker this time.

"Hey, we just gotta go out and play," Van said as he paced in front of his team in the locker room. That's right. We have a different team right now than we thought we had earlier, but let's just go out and play hard."

But as he was trying to give encouragement and inspiration to his nine healthy players who sat before him, his voice began to quiver and he stopped for a moment as Wanda's empty chair and locker slowly began to creep into sight. He had nine healthy players in front of him but he couldn't stop thinking about the one who couldn't be with them as they got set to play in this historic game.

"I got to thinking about how unselfish Wanda was and how much she wanted to play and how she wanted to be a part of this championship moment," he said. "Nobody in the room knew it, but I was really close to crying. Really, really close, and I fought off a lot of tears. I turned away for a moment and it just hit me, how much she meant to this team."

But his tears weren't about the odds that were now stacked against his team to win the inaugural WNBA championship; they were about a concern for a friend. He simply put the negatives aside and told his team to concentrate on what each player had to do. They, especially Jackson, responded.

Despite the Guyton situation, I was amazed at how calm Van was on championship day. Even he was amazed and still doesn't have an answer for it. All morning at his house, during breakfast, driving through traffic and upon arriving at Compaq Center, it seemed very normal to him. For twenty-eight regular-season games the guy was a bundle of nerves before a game. He watched more film, went over more substitution rotations, and paced more than any other coach I've ever been around.

It's a WNBA league policy that the locker rooms be open to the media ninety minutes before tip-off and close twenty minutes later. If the media miss the twenty-minute window, they're out of luck and they have to wait until post-game when the locker rooms reopen. Van hated to get to the arena early when we were on the road because he ended up twiddling his thumbs trying to find things to do before tip-off. Many times we would wait until the bitter end before leaving the hotel. It drove me crazy more than once, and there were several times when we would leave at 6:00 for a 7:30 tip. The locker rooms were supposed to open to the media at 6:00, and I knew we were in violation of league policy. On one of our early road trips during the first season, Van announced to the team at a luncheon that the bus would be leaving at 6:00. I immediately stood up and said, "Van, we can't do that. We're going miss the media availability."

"Well then, son, looks like we won't be talking to the media until after the game," he said. Good point, I thought, and I knew not to bring that subject up again.

In every NBA and WNBA arena, there are clocks in the locker rooms that have the countdown to tip-off. There were many nights when Van and his coaching staff would wait until under a minute before they would take the floor. Van was usually quite nervous and hated getting out to the court early with nothing to do. Before all nationally televised games on NBC, ESPN and Lifetime, Van would have me tie his necktie because frankly, by his own admission, Van's knots on his ties were larger than a *Krispy Kreme* pastry. But what amazed me most was when he would be nervous all day, wring his hands on the way to the arena on the bus and then promptly fall asleep after reading his Bible for a few moments. Sometimes he would just stay on the bus after everyone went inside, and take a nap in his seat. That was rare. Mostly he paced and talked.

But championship day was different. He was very calm and relaxed from start to finish—or at least he had everyone fooled into thinking he was relaxed. Van spends a lot of time talking with his coaching staff on the road, but at home he has his own office and locker room at Compaq Center. Normally he and Kevin Cook got ready in his small locker room, and it's a rather uneventful pre-game. On championship day, however, he had Betty, his wife of thirty-seven years, along with his son Johnny and Johnny's wife Angela in the room.

When Van talks about the longevity of his coaching career, he rarely uses the words "I" or "me." It's usually "we" or "us," in reference to Betty. She's been at Van's side since his coaching career began in 1965 and she helps him in so many ways—more than people realize. She's always in the background and doesn't say a lot at practices or games, but advises Van about so many other things when they get home. After the Comets won the inaugural championship game, Van told a group of media members that he and Betty had been coaching for thirty-three years, and winning it all was something they had always dreamed about. It seemed only appropriate that she should be with him prior to the biggest game of his, or should I say, their coaching career.

Tip-off for the championship game was at 1:30 P.M. and Van arrived at Compaq Center around 11:30, which was a little early for him. He usually liked to get to the arena about ninety minutes before tip, but on championship day he felt good and couldn't wait to get the day started. He woke up at about 6:30 and felt good about his team's chances against New York. When Van's ready to go it's best to absolutely drop everything you're doing and go with him or you'll get left behind. When he's ready to go it's time to go. In the Chancellor home during the basketball season, there isn't Central Standard Time, Mountain Standard Time or even Eastern Standard Time. There's Chancellor Standard Time and you'd better get to know it—early in the season.

He doesn't wait for anyone, including his own family. If you're running late on Chancellor Time, you're simply walking to the game. Van's father traveled from Louisville, Mississippi to Houston for the championship game and stayed with them the night before. He wasn't ready to go when Van was the next morning so Van left him with Betty back at the house. They had to fend for themselves to get to the arena. Van was ready to go!

It almost happened to me once, early in the first season at an exhibition game in Charlotte. Van told everyone to be on the bus at 5:30PM At 5:20 I came down from my room and I could sense I had about fifteen sets of eyeballs watching my every step as I made my way to the bus. There was nobody in the lobby of the hotel and I had a bad feeling as I stepped on board.

"Don't walk on this bus right now and think you're on time," he said. "When I'm ready to go is when the bus leaves."

He said it in a way that I didn't question his 5:30 deadline, which he had announced earlier in the day. The team

met at 5:15, and when the meeting adjourned early it was
time to go. I was always first on the bus after that.

❖

As game-time approached he spent more and more time
in the small locker room designated for his family. He wanted
to put everything aside and focus completely on the game.
One of his biggest problems that day was all the ticket
requests he had gotten from friends and colleagues. At one
point he told me he couldn't and didn't want to help anyone
else. It was absolutely overwhelming how big this game
had become for professional women's basketball and anyone who had ever vaguely spoken to Van in the past thirty
years was looking for tickets. He finally said "enough" and
retreated to the comforts of his family in his locker room.

I knew he didn't want to be bothered, but occasionally I
would check in on him to make sure he was all right and to
see if he or his family needed anything. "I'm doing all right,
son. But I sure do appreciate you checkin' in on us. How
you doin'? You keepin' up with everything?" he asked. I
smiled as I walked out of the locker room because I couldn't
believe he'd asked the question. The man was forty minutes
away from writing the history books, yet he remained calm,
was courteous and wanted to see if I was all right. In a
profession where egos can get in the way, Van seems to
overcome it and is as down-to-earth as anyone.

His final trip to the team locker room gave him comfort.
At the beginning of the season, one day before training
camp opened, we held a dinner at the team's practice facility,
Westside Tennis Club. It was the first time all the players
had a chance to meet with Van and all their new teammates.
As Van introduced each player, he handed her a fake diamond ring and told her to wear it until she could trade it in
for the real thing. As I walked with Van into the locker
room just minutes before tip-off, our players sat in their
chairs and a number of them had the fake diamonds on

their fingers. They told Van they were ready to make the trade. Van knew at that point there was something magical in the dressing room. From the time his team took the floor until the final buzzer sounded, Van felt confident, and that set it off.

He finally made his way to the floor a little after 1:00 to pass out his traditional candy. This ritual has definitely taken on a life of its own. Before every home game—heck, even road games now—Van makes his way around the arena with a bag of candy and throws it up into the stands. He even walks through airports passing out the stuff and there were a few occasions when all the passengers on our flight were treated by Van at thirty thousand feet. He did it on our first pre-season trip to Charlotte. After the plane got to a cruising altitude, Van stood up and said, "Hi, I'm Van Chancellor, head coach of the Houston Comets of the WNBA. Sure do hope y'all can come out on out and support us this year." My first thought was "Oh brother, what have I gotten myself into?" But as the first season went on, the fans came to appreciate it and so did I. What more could I ask for as a PR person? Harold Wiesenthal, from Harold's in the Heights, the man who outfitted Van on game days for a majority of his time in Houston, probably said it best when he told me after the season was over, "No disrespect to you, but I don't think Van needs a PR guy."

Hey, somebody had to tie his tie. But more than anything else, the candy toss, which is still going strong today, is a chance for Van to relax before games.

A 1:30 tip-off usually means teams don't have a shoot-around earlier in the day. If it were a night game, both teams would definitely have a shoot-around time in the morning. Although it was early, Van still decided to have a voluntary shoot-around at 8:00 AM., and most of his players were there to participate. New York failed to have a shoot-around because they had played their semifinal game in Phoenix on Thursday and didn't get into Houston until late in the afternoon on Friday. New York felt they would be better prepared by resting rather than having an early practice. Van felt that the Liberty had tipped their hand before the game ever started, as he sensed they were tired.

By not having an early-morning practice, Van thought the Comets could eventually wear them down in the second half. Flying from New York to Phoenix, playing a semifinal game and then flying from Phoenix to Houston all in about forty-eight hours fatigued their players, he thought. Van knew that under no circumstances should his team panic in the first half, because eventually New York would tire due to the travel.

❖

Eventually the candy was gone and it was time for the Comets to roll up their sleeves, spit in their hands and get after the New York Liberty. The arena had a pulse as 16,285 screaming fans got louder and louder just before player introductions. The frenzied fans were there to witness history in what was arguably the biggest game ever for professional women's basketball. Van's biggest battle, just moments before tip-off, was with his emotions. He was a veteran coach of thirty-three years; he had seen women's basketball come so far, he had to take a moment just to look around and see how many people had gathered to watch a professional women's basketball game in the United States. It had been a long time coming and Van had been a part of the sport's growth.

"I was so proud at that moment for women's basketball and the fans of Houston," he said. "It wasn't necessarily a good feeling for myself, but instead I felt proud to be a part of this game because the sport had been such a huge part of my life."

Player introductions were over and everyone's hearts were pounding a little faster; the butterflies had turned to bats in the pits of everyone's stomachs. It was incredibly loud just before the Comets took the floor, and Van sat with his team for the final time before they went out and made history. He looked his starting five in the face and reminded them of three things: "Hey, listen up now. Remember, number 1, we're at home, number 2, we'll take care of business at home and number 3, just play our game because we have the better team." That was it. Van knew we had the better team with better players. That was all the strategy he needed. Van's always said that the secret to good coaching is loading the bus with good players. Certainly this bunch made his life easier and made him look like a genius on more than one occasion.

He told them one last thing before they broke the huddle: "Play hard and the game will return to you—now go make history." Although the moment was intense and everyone was supposed to be concentrating on his or her assignments for the upcoming forty minutes of battle, that statement seemed to catch everyone for a moment. "Play hard and the game will return to you" is something Van has said throughout his coaching career as a motivator. It simply means don't get frustrated and don't let anything bother you because no matter what you do, if you give yourself enough opportunities, the game will return to you and you'll have a shot at winning. "Now go make history." Enough said.

It was a serious moment, and Van, always looking for a way to lighten the moment, could sense everyone was becoming a little overwhelmed. Van's not a serious guy, and anyone who's been around him very long can sense that almost immediately. It seemed like a heavy moment for the Comets as they broke huddle, so Van leaned over to Cynthia Cooper, the WNBA's Most Valuable Player and clearly one of the best players in the world, and said, "Hey, Coop, whatever you do, don't shoot an air-ball to open the game."

The player introductions were complete; the crowd raised

the decibel level in Compaq Center, Houston grabbed the opening tip and WNBA history books were in the process of being written. Houston's point guard, Kim Perrot, grabbed the opening tip and began to set up the offense. Her first pass to Cooper was kicked away by the WNBA Defensive Player of the Year, Theresa Weatherspoon. Nobody knew it at the time, but that opening pass was indicative of the way Perrot felt all day. She later told Van that the early stage of the game was the most nervous she had ever been in her life. What was perceived as a random kicked ball was actually a sign of the way Kim was feeling. Nerves were definitely a factor.

All day long, Van had no idea how nervous she was. Even after the game was over, Van and the coaching staff didn't know. They brought her into their offices several months after the season was over to show her some things they wanted her to work on during the off-season. They pointed out some things on the tape of the championship game that they wanted corrected for next year.

"I don't want you to think I'm making up excuses, but it's amazing that I actually made it through the entire game," Kim said of her nerves. Van had absolutely no idea she was feeling that way.

Kim did settle, however, and knocked down the first three-pointer of the game with 17:16 to play in the first half to give Houston an early 7-2 lead. They increased their early lead to nine when Cynthia Cooper scored on a seventeen-foot jumper to make it 19-10 with 9:31 to play. I'll never forget that moment after Cooper scored, looking up at the scoreboard and hearing the roar of the crowd. It started to really sink in that we might have a shot at winning this thing. I wanted to jump up and start talking to Van about everything, but I sat down with a lump in my throat, gripped my sweaty hands and hoped we could hang on.

Tammy Jackson's game was unbelievable. She grabbed

the first two defensive rebounds on New York's early posses-
sions and never looked back. Veterans just know how to get
it done in big games. Van had faith in her and knew she
would have a big game. Between Kevin Cook reminding him
about Jackson earlier in the day, and recalling Tammy's quote
in the paper about how good she felt in a match-up against
Hampton, Van felt comfortable with his inside game despite
the loss of Wanda.

Jackson is a thirteen-year veteran of professional women's
basketball and spent many years overseas. She graduated from
the University of Florida in 1985, after being named to the
All-SEC first team in three consecutive years. Van knew she'd
been in big games before, and a veteran of that many years
would get up for this contest.

In April 1997, when Van drafted her in the WNBA's inaugural draft in the second round (sixteenth pick overall), he
knew he was gambling on an older player. He was almost
talked out of the pick, but told everybody in the room, who
was helping him with the draft, "I like Jackson because she's
been around and played in some big games. We need a veteran post player and I think she fits into what I want to do.
End of story, let's move on to something else," he told the
group. He really said that because he wanted to start concentrating on the third round pick, but little did he know at that
time what a huge role she would play in helping bring the
first WNBA championship to Houston.

In that championship game, Van knew he had to play her
until she dropped. Houston needed a big game from her and
he knew she had to play the majority of the game. She finished the game having logged thirty-seven minutes, eighteen more than her season average. She also finished with a
team-high eleven rebounds. With 3:05 to play in the game,
she picked up her fifth foul and wisely played smart the remainder of the game. At that point, Houston was only up
50-43, and with Jackson out of the game due to fouls, the

Comets would have to rely on an untested bench during crunch time. Jackson's replacement, Yolanda Moore, came off the bench; her contribution during Houston's second championship season was tremendous, but during the 1997 season she had played in only thirteen games and had averaged just 7.2 minutes per game.

❖

Houston squandered its nine-point lead in the first half and took a 28-24 edge into halftime. Jackson had done her job against Hampton in the first half, as the center from New York was just 1-for-6 from the field. No surprise, Cynthia Cooper was the leading scorer with eleven, but still the Comets had blown a comfortable lead and were outscored 13-4 during one stretch in the first half when New York cut the lead to 23-22. However, to my surprise, Van wasn't upset or nervous during halftime, but was very confident in the locker room during the break.

"Let me tell ya, ladies; we're in good shape," he said as he walked around the room looking at a box score. "We held the New York Liberty to just twenty-four points in the entire first half. You just hang on for a few more minutes and get us any kind of a lead in the final minute and you're walking out of here World Champs."

I think at that point it really began to sink in for the players how close they really were. It was silent for a moment as everyone thought about it. I thought of how far this league and this team had come. Never in my wildest dreams would I have guessed how huge this thing was going to be. I never really cared much about women's basketball four months earlier, but now I wanted this team to finish out the half and let me be a part of something special. I thought about meeting Cynthia Cooper for the first time in March of 1997 when we made a public appearance in downtown Houston and no one knew who or what the Comets even were. Now, the Comets were just twenty minutes away from the WNBA's biggest prize and I knew *everyone* now knew who Cynthia Cooper was.

The second half opened and Hampton didn't stay quiet for long. The first two times the Liberty touched the ball in the second half she scored easily in the paint. That worried Van because he could see history repeating itself. Points in the paint were his biggest concern entering the game with the absence of Wanda on the floor, and this game looked frighteningly familiar to the first three times the Comets played New York in the regular season. In their three losses to New York, Houston led at halftime in every game.

"Oh, Lord, here we go again," was Van's first reaction. But he relaxed and called a quick timeout and told his team to try to put together a 'small run' to see if they could break New York. He had a feeling that if they could put together a little spurt they could distance themselves from New York for the rest of the half. It worked. After the Liberty cut the gap to two at 28-26 with 19:27 to play, Houston went on a burst and outscored New York 12-2 over the next six minutes and built a 40-28 lead. New York would get no closer than seven the rest of the way.

They got to within seven at 50-43 when Rebecca Lobo hit two free throws after Jackson was whistled with her fifth. It seemed to be New York's last chance to make a final run at Houston, so Van called a quick twenty-second timeout to settle his club. During the timeout Van ran a play for Cooper—could you blame him? He ran a lot of stuff Cooper's way the first year, and she was simply unstoppable for thirty straight games. If Cooper wasn't open, the ball was to go to Houston's Brazilian star, Janeth Arcain.

Houston needed a score coming out of the timeout and the play worked as Cooper was tightly guarded, but Arcain hit a nine-foot jumper with 2:36 to play that seemed to be the clincher. You could sense after that basket that New York had run out of steam and the threat was over.

Van felt comfortable about his defensive effort the entire forty minutes. Indeed, defense wins basketball games. At the very least, it won the inaugural WNBA Championship. But he was never at ease with his team on offense. Who would be? I don't think he was comfortable with that team on offense most of the year. Nearly one-third of Houston's shots during the regular season were three-pointers and they easily led the league in three-point attempts. On championship day the Comets were 4-of-14 from beyond the arc.

Van is an intense coach and he sometimes has a hard time relaxing during a game, even when the contest is securely in hand. The championship game was no exception. With fifty-one seconds left to play, Houston had a very comfortable lead and the noise level in Compaq Center was deafening. The players on the bench, assistant coaches and staff all began to realize that the first-ever WNBA championship belonged to Houston. The Comets led 60-47 with less than a minute to play, but Van didn't stop coaching because his biggest fear was letting it slip away. On a New York possession, Kim Perrot stole the ball and threw a razzle-dazzle, behind-the-back pass, as only Kim could do, on a fast break. It was one of those passes that drove Van crazy the entire season. Houston didn't capitalize on the play and they turned the ball over to New York. I was surprised when I saw Van nearly go through the roof because his team had a sure chance to score.

I think he was the only one in the building who didn't realize they had the game won. He jumped on Kim, and he knew immediately that he shouldn't have. The game was clearly over and she was just trying to add a little more excitement to an already incredible day. Van wasn't proud of himself and sat down on his chair on the bench and looked to the ceiling.

"Oh Van, don't be an idiot and just enjoy this," he said to himself.

"By the time we got the ball back and I looked at the

clock there were only 30 seconds left. That was the first time all day that I realized we had the game won and I could relax," he later said.

Moments later during a New York timeout, Van pulled Kim aside and apologized. But still, those passes gave Van more gray hairs than he wishes to count.

❖

As the final buzzer rang and the confetti flew at Compaq Center, it was an extremely emotional time. I knew I had a job to do, but it was difficult when Peggie Gillom and our equipment manager, Stacey Johnson, latched on for one of the loudest group hugs you can imagine. The place was going wild; chaotic is the best way to describe the first few moments after the game was over. I looked at Van and I could see every emotion in his face. He was so happy that he was overcome with tears. I realize Jimmy Valvano has the market on looking for someone to hug after winning a national championship, but Van was definitely lost for a moment. He was looking for Betty because he wanted to share this magical moment with the person who had been by his side for most of his life. Van's father, brother, son and daughter-in-law were also in the stands; his pride as a Chancellor was evident that day.

While searching for Betty, Van's thoughts turned to his mother and sister, both of whom had passed away years earlier. Even talking about it now makes this charismatic, intense and overpowering coach choke up. As WNBA history was made and everyone was grabbing at him and hugging him, Van stood silent for a moment and thought about his family, both those who could be at Compaq Center that Saturday and those who were certainly there in spirit.

Van found his wife, kissed her and embraced his entire family. A framed photograph of Van hugging his son hangs in the Chancellor home today. Shortly thereafter, Cynthia Cooper found Van and they embraced. Through the tears and the noise

I could still hear their conversation. "Thank you for making this happen for me," he said behind the tears. He certainly found the right person to thank for making that championship possible. It was an amazing few minutes following the game. I'll never forget the noise, the jubilation and the history that was being made. For a moment, time seemed to stand still.

The coaching profession is built on loyalty, and it's something that Van stands rock-solid upon. The Comets' training camp opened in May at Houston Baptist University. Near the University is an Olive Garden restaurant that Van went to nearly every day after practice. He continued to eat at the same restaurant for the entire season, long after training camp was over and the team wasn't near Houston Baptist any longer. Every time Van went back to the restaurant, they welcomed him and let Betty and him sit at the same spot. Van stills goes to the restaurant frequently, as it's a relaxing place for him following practice or a game. After Houston won the championship game and Van got through all the media requests and interviews, he was invited to the WNBA championship party at the Renaissance Hotel near Compaq Center. He joined his coaches and members of Houston's staff for a short time at the championship party, but Van has always said that it's a good idea to be true to the people who are true to you. He thought the people at the Olive Garden had treated him right all summer, and now it was time for him to treat them right by dining at their restaurant after the title game.

But before Van could join the championship party or get to the Olive Garden, we had several interview requests to fulfill. The last one was on Tim Melton's "Extra Point" show, Saturday afternoon on KTRH in Houston. The station sent a limousine to pick up Van and his family up at the arena. I walked with them to the limo and we talked briefly. He said something that I will never forget, because it truly measures his personality and ego. "Can you believe this, boy," he said. "I've always thought during this whole deal that I was just a part of it. I wasn't any more or any less than anyone on our team. By team I mean from the top down. From the people who sell the tickets, to the guy signing the checks, I'm just happy to be a part of this team. I know I'm not any more valuable than anyone else associated with this organization."

Van's always tried to remain humble after victories, but that drive up the tunnel out of Compaq Center and into a swarm of Comets fans seemed to be just too much. He had the limo driver stop and open the roof, and he stood out of the top and waved to the screaming fans. He signed a few autographs, and the limo slowly drove away. His dad was also with him in the limo. Van knew his dad was proud, but he didn't want to show it. Van sat back down after waving to the fans, and the entire limo was laughing and having a great time. Van's dad said, "Son, you'll always be a cotton farmer from Mississippi to me, now sit down!"

I was scheduled to meet Van the next morning at 7:00 A.M. at Westside Tennis Club, where we would begin a long day of interviews with national media people. History was made that day; Van was the head coach of the first WNBA championship team and it caught the attention of every national news organization in the country. But the tragic death of Princess Diana the same night bumped Van from any national television appearances the following day. In the midst of the most exciting day of his life, a day he had dreamed about for so long, Van realized it was still just a game and that there were more important things to deal with in this world.

Instead of meeting with me and making our rounds on the national television circuit, I had to call Van at 1:00 A.M. to tell him that all interviews were off.

It's just a basketball game—I understand, son. Lord knows I understand.

POST-GAME PRESS CONFERENCE
WNBA FINALS—AUGUST 30, 1997

VAN'S OPENING REMARKS: "When I moved to Houston, Texas, I never spent a day that I didn't dream about winning the WNBA Championship and about how nice it would be. After getting here, it's sweeter than I'd ever dreamed it would be from a personal point of view. I'm so proud of our players. What an effort today from Tammy Jackson, what an effort from everybody on our team. When we lost Wanda Guyton I thought we'd have trouble. I can't say enough about our defensive effort. When we came here, we opened up training camp on defense and that was our emphasis, and what a game."

Q: "Can you talk a bit about Tina's (Thompson) effort today?"

Van: "Tina Thompson had eighteen points. The luckiest move I made was on the night before the draft; I couldn't make up my mind between Tina Thompson and another player. Les Alexander called me and said, "Hey, we don't have Sheryl (Swoopes), I don't know if we can win a championship. Go young, I'll stay with you." When Les told me that, we went young and thank God we did. What a choice. She had eighteen points and I thought she was outstanding on Rebecca Lobo tonight. Defensively, I think she's one of the most underrated players in this league."

Q: "How about Tammy Jackson's play?"

Van: "Tammy Jackson came in and never blinked an eye. She started the biggest game of her life after not playing big minutes and played thirty-seven minutes. That's a test to her character, her intestinal fortitude and everything else. What a game."

Q: "How does it feel to be the first coach to ever win the WNBA?"

Van: "I'll tell ya, a team coach should never be dealing in individualities, but this feels good. I'd by lying if I said it didn't. You have to understand, I came so close four times on the other team's home court as a college coach and getting into big games in the Final Four, and I never could make it. I just wanted to win."

Van's closing remarks: "This has been a thrill of a summertime. I'm about as happy today as I've ever been in my life. I don't want to say it's better than the day I got married thirty-five years ago because I have my wife with me, but it's darn close, I'll tell you that right now. Let me tell you my thinking there. You can get married a lot of days; you can't win a championship every day. You agree with that? She'll kill me tomorrow."

Chapter 2
Raising A Champion

THERE WAS ONLY ONE THING worse for Van than getting up in the morning as a young boy and realizing that his day was going to be filled with picking cotton under the hot, steamy Mississippi sun. And that was actually getting to the field to pick cotton under the hot, steamy Mississippi sun.

Van's got one of the strongest work ethics of anyone I've ever met, and it was fine-tuned as a child on the family farm in Louisville, Mississippi. He really didn't have a choice but to have a strong work ethic, as his dad, Winston Chancellor, ran a fairly tight ship on the family's cotton farm. The Chancellors didn't have a lot, and everything they did have was a result of a lot of hard work each summer. They lived in a small area about seven miles outside of the Louisville city limits called the Nanih Waiya Community. Van's dad owned 400 acres of land, and although he had several interests on the farm, cotton was the main source of the family's income.

Although the Chancellors were big basketball fans while he was growing up, Van's dad and brother, Hezekiah, spent most of their time working, hunting or fishing. The stick and ball sports never grabbed the attention of his family the way they did for Van. Money was hard to come by in the Chancellor home so his parents couldn't provide a lot of the extras. But the most important thing they gave Van was a strong work ethic and a lot of love, neither of which cost a dime.

As Van puts it, his family farmed cotton the old-fashioned way, not the way they do things now. They farmed with hoes to eradicate the weeds, whereas today cotton farmers use chemicals. When it was harvest time, Van and his family joined the hired hands on the farm and they picked the cotton; they didn't use an automatic picker, as is used today. Van's dad worked him as hard as he's ever been worked in his life, every day, no questions. He believed in hard work and that the only way to get ahead in life was to get up early, put in an honest day's work and do it all over again the following day. Van's father actually worked in Louisville at the United States Department of Agriculture, which is why he needed Van and the hired help during the day, because the work in the field fell to the family. And after spending a long day at the USDA, Winston joined Van at night and they'd work for many hours into the evening.

Farming was a way of life in Louisville, and the people in the area didn't stray far from the farm. To break the monotony of daily chores, Louisville natives did one of two things. If they weren't fishing, they were hunting. Everyone in the community loved the outdoors and spent nearly all their idle time participating in one of these two sports. But the attraction to the outdoors and the sports it provided never excited Van.

"My daddy took me out to a deer-hunting stand one day and I never did see a deer—not all day long," Van said. "I've never been huntin' since."

Van's only outlet from the incredible amount of hard work put on him at the farm was basketball. He had a passion for it and couldn't wait to see it, read about it or play it. Granted, the family didn't have a lot, but his parents always made sure he had a solid basketball goal, an adequate rim, a net and a basketball on the front lawn for Van to play with. Even though Winston pushed Van harder than anyone has ever since, he enjoyed watching him play ball and always made sure that he had enough equipment to play every day.

The front yard of the Chancellor home looked more like Madison Square Garden than it did the yard of a modest cotton farmer from Mississippi. Fortunately for Van, the front yard had just a few patches of worn grass while the rest of the surface was covered in dirt that had turned rock-hard after being baked in the Mississippi sun. Van built two goals in the yard, and created a court by taking a cotton hoe and digging in the dirt to form the appropriate lines resembling an official court. It certainly wasn't the best outdoor basketball court in the land, but to Van it was the only one that mattered.

Every night after he finished his chores, Van headed out-side to shoot on his hoe-made basketball court. Just like every kid in America playing in a front driveway, Van played out several games and had several different fantastic fin-ishes as the crowd went wild. There's no question that he single-handedly won the Mississippi High School State Championship in his head several times on the front lawn.

Even today when he speaks to students at school assem-blies or clinics, he reaches back to his childhood days to get the message across about hard work and a positive attitude. He had to work hard on the farm in Louisville, but he always kept a positive attitude. Every night before he called it quits on the front lawn, he went through the same sce-nario where he got one last shot at the buzzer for the win. If the final shot went in at the buzzer, that was it, Van had to fight his way inside his house with hundreds of imagi-nary fans grabbing at him and asking for an autograph. If the final shot rattled out, it was obvious that he was fouled. If the foul shot didn't go down, then someone from the opposing team was called for a lane violation and he got another shot from the charity stripe. Every night he played this game and every night he won. Play until you win—not a bad game.

❖

As Van grew older he became more interested in sports and played just about every sport he could get his hands on. Van and his childhood buddies played football, baseball, basketball and any other game they could think of, but his passion always returned to basketball. When he entered Louisville High School, he continued to play every game he could with his friends, but basketball and track were the only two sports he competed in competitively. The main reason he played so many sports is because it gave him a break from all the chores back home on the farm.

"My dad was beginning to simply work the life out of me," Van said. "Every morning we'd get up and milk the cows. If we weren't milking the cows, we were working in the fields. If we weren't working in the fields, we were working in the garden. If we weren't working in the garden, we were hauling hay. If we weren't hauling hay, we were choppin' cotton. If we weren't choppin' cotton, we were pickin' cotton. If we weren't pickin' cotton, we were clearing the pasture lines. If we weren't clearing the pasture lines, we were fixin' fences. If we weren't fixin' fences, we were moving hay from one side of the barn to the other for no apparent reason. All I could think about was getting off that farm. I finally started to realize that if I played ball I could get out of some of that work."

One winter night (granted, a Mississippi winter night isn't the worst thing in the world, but nonetheless it was still a winter night), Van missed his ride after practice and walked nearly three miles home from school. He was miserably cold by the time he got home but at least he knew by that hour he would get out of his nightly chores. He felt bad because he knew his dad would end up doing them, but at least he thought he had gotten out of chores for a night. He walked in the door, apologized to his mom and was confident he had a night off. A sad look came over her face as she saw Van standing pathetically in the doorway. She told him that his dad had gone duck hunting and that he would still need to head to the barn to milk the cows. Van was cold, crying and certainly unwilling to do the task. With his mother's help, they completed the chores; but that was the last time for Van. Van's mother, Wanda, stepped in and put a stop to it.

Winston ran a rather tough program on their farm until Wanda stepped in. She told Van's dad that he would either have to start milking the cows in the afternoon or else Van would have to stop playing basketball for the high school. Winston loved to watch Van play and he accepted Wanda's ultimatum. That particular order helped pave the way to Van's basketball success; he could practice as long as he liked after school from then on.

The fantasy games in the front yard of his youth quickly turned to the real thing as he landed a spot on the Louisville varsity team. Van will be the first to admit that he never saw a shot he didn't like in high school. If he touched it, he shot it. Early in his senior season his head coach, Gary Hughes, pulled Van aside and told him that he needed to shoot the ball more in order for Louisville to be successful. He was the only senior on the team and played on a starting lineup that consisted of two sophomores, a junior and a freshman. Being the only senior on the club, he took Hughes' comments to heart.

"Back in those days, if a coach told you to run through a brick wall you ran through the wall," Van said of his coach's instructions. "You didn't stop and say, 'Hey coach, do you think that wall might hurt?' So when he told me I had to shoot more, I took it seriously and really began to fire up a lot of shots."

One night in Dekalb, Mississippi, Van shot the ball thirty-three times and scored twenty-six points. They got beat, or should I say Van got beat, since he was the only one who touched the ball. As the team got off the bus that night, Hughes put his arm around Van and sarcastically said, "Van, I know I told ya to shoot the ball more, but Good Lord."

Van averaged twenty-three points per game for the Wildcats of Louisville and had a fairly decent high school career. His goal was always to play in the state tournament in Jackson, and as a sophomore he got the chance. Van was the first substitute during that season and though they got beat in the state tournament, he played three minutes, which up to that point was the highlight of his basketball career. The fact that the Wildcats even made it to the state tournament in Jackson that year is amazing. Early in his sophomore year, the gymnasium in Louisville burned to the ground and the team was forced to practice on a dirt court while the rest of the schools in the state were practicing in regular gymnasiums. The problem was never solved while Van was in high school; he practiced on a dirt court his entire career at Louisville and never played a home game his junior or senior year.

In high school Van's interests were girls, lunch and basketball—and lunch was the least favorite of the three. He didn't take his studies too seriously and he hated doing his chores back on the farm, but he loved to play basketball. But because he spent so much time on the basketball court and not enough time with his nose in a schoolbook, he was in quite a mess following his senior year. He had four fun-filled years at Louisville, but when the basketball ended after graduation in 1961, the only thing staring back at him was a lifetime in a steamy cotton field in central Mississippi. The thought of spending the rest of his life sweating in a cotton field scared him.

He felt certain he had more to give than sweat and tears. One summer day following his senior year at Louisville, he baked in the hot, humid sun. He was seventeen years-old with a heart filled with dreams and hopes when he looked to the sky and said, "Lord, if you'll just let me get out of this cotton field, I'll *never* come back. Please help me get to college, I promise I'll study and I'll get my degree."

Peggie Gillom, Van's assistant for many years, says that Van is the most blessed person she's ever met. That day in Mississippi could very well have been the first of many because he's never been back to work on the farm and has no intentions of starting again.

With high school behind him and the first of several prayers answered, Van headed to East Central Junior College in Decatur, Mississippi, on a basketball scholarship. His scholarship was half basketball and half work-study, which meant he was required to sweep the gymnasium floor every day. At East Central, Van was the self-proclaimed All-time Greatest Junior College benchwarmer in the history of junior college basketball. He never played—never—not a lick. He was the twelfth man on an eleven-man roster, and the head coach, Denver Brackeen, kept one seat open on the end of the bench just in case somebody in the stands was better than Van.

The 119-pound scrawny freshman entered junior college with fire in his eyes as he looked forward to continuing his playing career. He knew he wasn't good enough to play anywhere else, and the fact that basketball had taken him out of the cotton fields for another year excited him. But as the games continued and the minutes weren't there, Van realized that his playing days were coming to a close. He went to East Central for one reason. It wasn't for an education and it wasn't solely to play basketball; it was to get off the farm. But after a week of being in school, he looked around and saw that college life wasn't too bad—it didn't matter if he was shooting jump shots or not. He knew it was time to buckle down and educate himself so he would never have to return to the fields again. He went to school hoping for a one-year reprieve from tough work, and learned that if he applied himself he could get a lifetime reprieve.

At least he got that much out of junior college because playing basketball was one of the biggest disappointments of his life. In the very last game during the playoffs his second year at East Central, Van's club was getting beat by thirty-two points and he was the only player on the team who didn't get off the bench. He had a hard time understanding that, but he kept his mouth shut and stayed loyal. Loyalty is such a big part of coaching, and though Van was young and still learning, it was in his best interest to stay loyal. He realizes now that his loyalty to Denver Brackeen paid off for him as Brackeen helped Van land a major high school coaching job in Mississippi a few years later.

Life takes many twists and turns and it's easy to look negatively on situations that arise in our lives. The fact that Van labored most of his life and then hardly played at East Central didn't discourage him. It gave him a stronger work ethic than most. He doesn't rely on anyone else but himself. When he first took the job in Houston, he was up at the crack of dawn every day trying to help sell the Comets. He worked more hours than most on the Comets staff and the fifty-four-year-old had as much enthusiasm about the WNBA as did anyone in the country. He didn't rest; he never has.

❖

Ironically, Van was a huge fan of the Mississippi State men's basketball program when he was a child. The Bulldogs are bitter rivals with the Rebels of Ole Miss, the place Van spent the majority of his coaching career. The family farm in Louisville was thirty minutes from Starkville and the campus of Mississippi State University. He and his dad used to jump in the car, drive to Starkville for a men's basketball game, wait for the game to start, and then sneak in the backdoor of the gymnasium. In 1959 he saw Mississippi State, coached by Babe McCarthy, play Kentucky, led by Adulf Rupp, and can vividly remember Hall-of-Famer Bailey Howell and Kermit Davis battling the Wildcats at the Bulldogs' old 5,000-seat Newell Grissom Fieldhouse.

Howell went on to be one of the greatest players in Mississippi State history and was drafted by the Detroit Pistons in the first round of the 1959 NBA draft. He helped guide the Boston Celtics to the 1968 and 1969 NBA championships and averaged 18.7 points and 9.9 rebounds per game over his twelve-year NBA career. Van has since become friends with Bailey, and that game in 1959 remains one of Van's greatest sporting memories while growing up in Mississippi. Van's bottom jaw was on the floor every time he went to Starkville to watch the Bulldogs. He knew from that point that one of his goals in life was to be on the coaching staff at Mississippi State.

He knew he wasn't good enough to play at Mississippi State—he'd had a hard enough time keeping his legs from cramping while sitting on that bench at East Central. So he thought the next best thing was to be a coach there. When he was in high school, he couldn't decide if the Lord wanted him to be a preacher or a coach. Van's Sunday School teacher in high school, Marquerite Fulton, saw how confused and concerned he was and said, "Van if you don't feel that God is calling you into the ministry; just think about it and remember that you can minister to a lot of young people as a coach. Maybe that's your calling."

Those days on the campus of Mississippi State got Van's juices flowing for big-time basketball. His ultimate dream job was to become an assistant men's coach for the Mississippi State Bulldogs. Today, he wouldn't touch the job and has no regrets about never coaching in Starkville.

❖

After spending two seasons at East Central, Van continued his education at Mississippi State and received his bachelor's degree in mathematics. Without the degree in math Van probably wouldn't have gotten his first high school coaching job at Noxapater High School, in Noxapater, Mississippi. A math teacher/basketball coach was a hot commodity in 1965 and Noxapater was in a bind. The school offered Van the head coaching position while he was still a senior in college.

During a break from school while a senior at Mississippi State, Van was with his family in Louisville when he received a phone call from Thomas Satterfield, the principal at Noxapater. Satterfield offered Van $3800 to come to Noxapater to teach math and to coach the boys basketball team. Van turned it down because of money, but the next day they called back and offered him $4800. "Hey, I was a rare breed in 1965," he said. "I could coach basketball and teach mathematics and I think that's why they offered me the extra $1000 per year."

Van and Betty were married when he was still a sophomore in college. Betty had worked to put Van through four years of college and the only reason Van accepted the Noxapater position was because he felt it was his time to start providing for his family. So Van took the $4800 and the boy's basketball-coaching position, and began what would ultimately become, ironically, a long, storied career in coaching women's basketball.

Van's grateful for his time in his dad's cotton fields. While he was there he was as ungrateful as a human being could possibly be. But his parents taught him the true meaning of hard work and gave him a true definition of a strong work ethic. If nothing else, it helped Van appreciate the blessing of being accepted into college, and it gave him the drive to educate himself. For a family that concentrated more on farming, hunting and fishing, Van's parents gave him every opportunity to explore his interests when he was a child.

For my parents to provide so many opportunities and back me in my choice of basketball, I'm forever thankful.

Chapter 3
Learning the Craft

VAN WAS AT NOXAPATER for two years and by no means did he set the world on fire. He's been in coaching for thirty-four years and only once did he coach a team to a losing record—his first. Noxapater went 8-20 during his rookie campaign as head coach and 14-14 the second season.

In his first game in 1965 at the age of twenty-one, Van's Noxapater Tigers played Edinberg, Mississippi. Van was so ready for his first game that he could hardly concentrate throughout the day. He was young, full of spunk, had great ideas and was ready to outsmart any coach who thought he could get in his way. The entire day of the game he continued to tell himself that he was a coaching machine and that he had all the answers for everything Edinberg had to dish out. At that age you think you're invincible, and Van was certain that he was. He felt ready to take the basketball coaching profession by storm and was determined to take Mississippi High School basketball to a new level. But the players and coaches of Edinberg didn't quite see Van's angle, and humiliated Noxapater 74-29.

"Pahdnah, in a span of about two hours, Edinberg High School and the good Lord humbled me as fast as you can humanly be humbled," Van said about his introduction to the coaching ranks. He walked to school the next morning and thought to himself, 'This sure is a big world, but you'd be hard pressed to find a worse coach than I am.' It was one of the more humbling experiences of his life—thankfully it came at the very beginning.

The loss to Edinberg wasn't the worst of it. During the game, someone broke into Van's trailer home, which was parked behind the gym, and stole what was then his most prized possession. Heck, it would be his most prized possession today: his TV. He and Betty didn't have a lot in 1965 and he knew there was absolutely no way they could afford a new one. "I got beat by fifty points and some joker stole my TV," he said. "The good Lord was definitely testing me that night."

The next day Van and Betty were at his parents' house for Sunday dinner and Van was still extremely down on himself. Van isn't the best loser on the planet. He wasn't in 1965, and things haven't improved with age. Late in the afternoon, he got a phone call from E. L. Vowell, chairman of the Noxapater School Board and father of the team's star player. He asked Van to meet with him and the rest of the board at the school at 5:00.

Van swallowed hard and slowly put the phone down, certain he was going to get fired after just one game. Needless to say, his self-confidence was at an all-time low. Were they going to fire him because of his conduct on the sidelines, he wondered. Were they going to get rid of him because of how badly they got beat, or because he ran Vowell's son, David, out of practice a day earlier because Van didn't think he was playing as hard as he could. All these things were running through Van's mind on the way to Noxapater's gymnasium. It didn't matter which way they fired him, he thought, he just knew he was going to get fired.

With heavy hearts, Van and Betty walked to the car with newly born Johnny in hand and headed for certain doom. As they drove closer to the school, the number of parked cars increased and they realized there were more people attending this meeting than just five school board members. "Oh brother, this is going to be a lynching," Van thought to himself. He was convinced all of the players' parents were in on the meeting as well.

Van entered the school with sweaty palms and thoughts of a new career on his mind. But as he walked into Vowell's office, he couldn't believe what he saw. He didn't get the greeting he expected, and what he thought would be scowls were actually smiles. Vowell was a man of few words, but he grabbed Van, pulled him into the office so everyone could see him and said, "Coach, we know you're going to bring this team around. We all have confidence in you, just stay on these guys and we'll all be okay. We also know your television was stolen last night and we wanted you to have this new one."

"I learned an important lesson that night in Noxapater," Van said. "People are good, and the best asset a coach can have is parents who support him or her. I was tougher on those kids at Noxapater than any other team I've ever coached. But they responded to this coach who was only a couple of years older than them. Most importantly, they responded and some of them are my best friends today."

❖

Noxapater was in the smallest class of high school basketball in Mississippi, and after two years of struggling at a school with 150 students, Van knew he was ready for more. He was ready to win and he just didn't feel he could get it done at a small school like Noxapater. In order to win, Van knew he needed to get to a larger school where the talent pool was bigger.

In Mississippi in the late 1960s, there were four classes of high school basketball: Class BB, which included Noxapater and the smallest schools in the state, Class B, Class A and Class AA, which included the biggest schools in Mississippi. The normal progression for a coach in a Class BB school obviously would be to jump to a Class B school. However, Van caught a break in 1967: he made the unheard of leap from a Class BB school to a Class AA school when he was offered the head coaching position at Horn Lake High School. Horn Lake had an enrollment of about 800 students—a school of gigantic proportions in 1967.

The Horn Lake job had a domino effect on the rest of Van's coaching career. If Van hadn't been named the head coach at Horn Lake in 1967, he wouldn't be in Houston today. He made a giant leap from a BB school to an AA school and had success at Horn Lake. That success enabled him to be offered bigger and better positions as his coaching career continued. Horn Lake was a break, no question, but he used that break to his fullest advantage. Van also took on a new responsibility at Horn Lake as he began coaching both the boy's and girl's teams. Over seven seasons he compiled an impressive mark of 337-103 (164-51 boys, 173-52 girls).

Van didn't have any business getting the Horn Lake job, which makes it even more ironic in the development of his career. In 1967 he was a nobody with a losing record. He wasn't a former college superstar, and no one in Mississippi knew who he was, so landing a coaching position at Class AA Horn Lake at the age of twenty-three, with a combined record of 22-34, was unthinkable. However, once he heard of the opening and the thoughts of coaching at a larger school raised his interest, he immediately called the school's principal, John Caldwell.

Mr. Caldwell told Van there was absolutely no way he would be able to offer him the job because he was too young and didn't have nearly enough experience. Van knew math teachers were in high demand and he told Caldwell that he had a math degree from Mississippi State and that he also once played for Denver Brackeen at East Central Junior

College. Although Van sat on the bench for two years for Coach Brackeen at East Central, he knew that having stayed loyal to him over those two agonizing years might now pay off.

Brackeen was an All-American at Ole Miss in the 1950s and was later drafted by the New York Knicks in 1955. Caldwell was a student at Ole Miss during Brackeen's time with the Rebels and he always kept up on his career. When Caldwell got off the phone with Van about the Horn Lake position, he called Coach Brackeen and asked him what he thought about 'this Chancellor kid.' Brackeen told him that Van sat on his bench for two years and never got to play, but that he never griped and never had a bad attitude. He basically told Caldwell that Van at least deserved a shot at an interview.

Van's phone rang later in the day after he had talked with Caldwell about the position. It was Denver Brackeen, someone Van hadn't talked with since leaving East Central. He told Van not to get nervous, but he thought he might have a shot at the Horn Lake position. Van didn't believe it, and went to the interview in Horn Lake with absolutely no confidence because he knew he wasn't qualified. But at least Coach Brackeen had gotten him the interview—and probably a whole lot more.

After Van offered the information to Caldwell that he could teach algebra along with the pick 'n' roll, the principal's interest increased. He told Van he could come to Horn Lake for an interview but not to expect anything. Apparently being able to teach math in Mississippi in the 1960s raised a few eyebrows when you were out job-hunting. So Van and Betty jumped into the car and headed north to Horn Lake, about ten miles south of Memphis, Tennessee, on the very northern tip of Mississippi. The Memphis area is a hotbed for hoops, and Van was excited.

As he and Betty cruised up Interstate 55 towards Horn

Lake, Van started to get a little worried. Keep in mind, Van's a country boy who'd never been too far from home and the thought of living clear up in the northern part of the state concerned him. They got to Batesville, just south of Horn Lake, and it felt like the other end of the world. Van wasn't sure he could handle living that far from home. When he looks back on it now, he's amazed he was able to make that big a move, so far from his mom and dad.

It was obvious upon his arrival that Caldwell was just throwing Van a bone and had no intention of offering him any type of job. As Van walked around the high school campus and saw the nice new athletic facilities and some of the prospective players, he knew he wanted the position. Caldwell was giving Van the standard tour of the facilities and the school. He was even giving him the standard interview and Van could tell it was going nowhere. He had to make a move because he didn't want to let this palace of a school get out of his grasp.

The rest of the story as Van tells it:

About fifteen minutes into the interview and guided tour, Van stopped Caldwell.

"I just wanna let you know—if you offer me this job, I'm takin' it," Van told him. Caldwell grinned and kept walking. "I'm serious," Van said. "If you offer me this job today, I'm gonna take it."

Caldwell replied, "Coach, I just can't offer you this job."

"I know that's what you're saying," Van replied. "I'm just tellin' ya that if you do offer me this job, I'm takin' it—I just want you to know that."

Caldwell shook his head and grinned as he continued the tour and made small talk. He still didn't show a lot of interest.

"Mr. Caldwell, if you offer me this job, I'm gonna take it," Van said again, about ten minutes later.

"Son, you don't even know what it pays," he said with a smile on his face.

"I don't care what it pays—if you offer me this job I'm gonna take it."

Later, as the day and interview were winding down, Van said for the fourth and fifth time, "I hate to interrupt, but if you offer me this job today, I'm gonna take it." Finally, Caldwell stopped, turned to Van and said, " I'm gonna tell you for the last time, I am not offering you this job, now please, quit asking."

"That's fine," Van said immediately. "But if you did decide to ever offer me this job, I'm gonna take it—today, right now."

"You haven't even talked to your principal," Caldwell said.

"I don't care what it pays, if you offer me this job, I'm gonna take it," Van said for the eighth time.

"Well this job doesn't pay but $4800 per year. What's that do for you?" Caldwell asked.

"That's a $100 per year pay cut for me," Van said. He was now making $4900 at Noxapater after a $100 pay raise in the second year of his contract.

"That not bother you, to take a pay cut to come coach here?" Caldwell asked with a grin and a bewildered look on his face.

"I done told ya for the last time, if you offer me this job, I'm gonna take it," Van said, his grin matching Caldwell's.

"Well, son, you have just come in here and worn me down," Caldwell said. "I have never seen anybody want a job so bad. Could you please just tell me why you want to be here so badly?"

"First of all, I'm moving a long way from my mom and dad to be up here and I'd be moving my wife from her mom and dad to come here, but I want to win," Van said. "I ain't coming here but to do one thing, and that's win."

"Well I've got a local school board member who lives right near the school. Let's go see him just in case I might want to offer you this job at some point," Caldwell said, and

Van could feel the door opening slightly. That's the way it is with Van—you open the door slightly and he'll blow the hinges off.

Van really laid it on heavy for Caldwell and the school board member, Ray Wooten. He told them that he knew he didn't have any experience and that he wasn't a great coach today, but he also knew that the Horn Lake program had to grow and that he needed to grow. "I think if we can grow together that in three years we could be really good," Van told the two.

"Could you maybe cut that down to two years," Wooten asked, seriously.

"I can get it down to six weeks," Van said in an excited voice. After he said that they asked him to step outside, and he knew he'd either clinched the deal or killed it. Driving all the way to Horn Lake was a gamble so he figured he might as well let it ride.

Van made his way back to the car where Betty had been waiting patiently during the entire interview. Betty is still that way, always gracious, always patient, in the background and always supportive of everything Van does. He sat down in the car, obviously mentally exhausted, and gave this piece of great insight: "Well, they're either gonna say yes or no."

Betty and Van sat and talked for what seemed to be forever, before they finally saw Caldwell make his way out of the school and toward the 1959 Plymouth. "Well, son, if I did offer you this job, do you want to go home and tell your principal about it?" he asked.

Van paused, looked at the steering wheel and grinned when he looked back up at Caldwell. "Mr. Caldwell, I've been telling you over and over again for the past hour that if you offer me this job, I'm gonna take it. Everybody I need to talk to is sittin' in this car with me."

With that, Caldwell offered Van the job and he had a feeling he was on his way to a long career in coaching if he could make this one work. On a day when the principal and the Horn Lake school board had no intentions of offering their head coaching position to a twenty-three-year-old kid with a losing record, Van convinced them it was the right move to hire him. Caldwell granted Van the interview as a gesture to Denver Brackeen, but Van made it happen.

"Please do me a favor," Caldwell said after offering Van the job. "Do not bug me any more tonight about this job. Can we please just talk about how you're gonna turn this program around?"

Van felt like the pressure was already on but he didn't mind. He knew he was in the big-time now: the Class AA schools took this whole winning thing seriously and that was right where he wanted to be.

"I wanna practice in the summer, heck, I wanna practice all the time," Van told him. "Well get up here June 1 and I'll give you the keys to the gym and you can have at it," Caldwell replied.

Van shook his hand, got back in the car and headed back to Noxapater. He knew he'd accomplished something that day, but had no idea at the time how gigantic a step this was in his coaching career. Denver Brackeen's name and phone conversations with John Caldwell helped that day and it was Van's first lesson in staying loyal in coaching. His loyalty to Coach Brackeen paid off and it should be the foundation for every coach today. Many times in today's game, players aren't happy with so many things and they start to complain. For every Michael Jordan there has to be a tenth man. Van was that tenth man for two long seasons at East Central, but it all came back to help him in the end.

In October of 1997, after the Comets had won their first of three championships, Van was inducted into the East Central Junior College Athletic Hall of Fame and went back to Decatur to accept his award. Every starter from his team was in attendance; the same guys who played while

Van was sitting on the bench. "Can you believe the irony in this, fellas?" Van said to the crowd when he was at the podium. "Back in school I had to watch you guys play while I sat there all night on the bench. Now the greatest benchwarmer in the history of basketball is up here accepting this award while you five starters are sitting on the bench—I mean in the audience!"

❖

Van kept his promise to Caldwell and Wooten about taking Horn Lake to the state tournament in Jackson. They had success, both with the boy's and girl's teams: Horn Lake had nine state tournament appearances in Van's seven years. Although he didn't quite get it done in six weeks like he told them in his initial interview, they still made tremendous strides early. In his first season with the Eagles, the boy's team finished with a record of 25-7 and missed the state tournament by one game. In the second year, however, both the boy's and girl's teams made it to the state tourney.

Although Van never coached a team to a state championship at Horn Lake, they came close many times. 1971 was probably the best shot at winning a state title for both the boy's and girl's teams, but Van fell short. The way both of his seasons ended in 1971 would make the strongest of men weep.

When coaches get beat at the buzzer, it can put them in a funk that will last for days, sometimes weeks, sometimes months, and sometimes forever. In 1971 Van lost two buzzer-beaters on the same day in two separate state tournament games, which brought his season to a crashing close. In the afternoon, Van's boy's team from Horn Lake got beat by one point at the horn in the first round of the tournament at the Jackson Coliseum. That team certainly wasn't his greatest at Horn Lake, but all season long the players kept assuring Van that they would get to the state tournament. In their last regular-season game, they got beat by thirty-seven points but came on strong in the post-season and qualified for the tournament, only to get beat at the buzzer in the opening round.

Immediately following the gut-wrenching buzzer-beater in Jackson, Van skipped the post-game speech and headed for a waiting highway patrol car, which carted him off to Pearl, Mississippi, five miles east of Jackson. His girl's team was playing in the state semifinal game in Pearl, and he didn't get to the gym until the end of the first quarter. In 1971 they didn't wait for the coach before tip-off. It didn't matter if you coached both the boys and girls teams—you were on your own to get to the arena on time. The highway patrolman gave Van some early gray hairs on the way, as they were flat-out flying on their way to Pearl. Van's girl's team that season was solid. They were definitely favored in the semifinal game and many thought they'd be playing for a state title. But one of the longest days of Van's career just continued to grow uglier as the girls also fell victim to a buzzer-beater and lost by two points.

"That day was one of the lowest points of my professional career, and the night was one of the longest of my life up until my mother died unexpectedly," Van said of the two buzzer-beaters in a matter of hours. "We had some good teams but just didn't have enough to win it all. I began to doubt myself as a coach and I just didn't know if I could win the big game."

When Van graduated from Mississippi State, his goal was to become a head coach—he got that at Noxapater. His next goal was to get to the state tournament—he got that at Horn Lake. His final goal was to win the state championship—it was time for a new school.

❖

Although Van was never able to win a state championship at Horn Lake, he certainly made up for it while he was at Harrison Central High School in Lyman, Mississippi. Harrison Central is another Class AA school, but the enrollment there was 1600 students, one of the ten biggest in the state. He took the head-coaching job for the boy's and girl's teams at Harrison Central in 1973 for an annual salary of $7000, an increase of $1000 per year from his final season at Horn Lake.

The Harrison Central job was one he had wanted for a long time because he really felt he had a better shot at winning a state title at a school that size. Two years earlier, in 1971, he interviewed for the head job at Harrison Central with athletic director Howard Patton, but at that time he stayed at Horn Lake because he felt a real loyalty to the school and John Caldwell for giving him his first real break.

However, in 1973, when the position opened again, Van still had a lot of interest and he thought it was a good time to move his family to Lyman. He was scheduled to interview with Patton at 1:00 on a spring afternoon in 1973, but Van was late and didn't arrive in Lyman until 1:30. The high school cafeteria was shut down for the afternoon but Patton was able to talk the ladies in the cafeteria into reopening so he and Van could have lunch. Van felt that he really wanted to work for a guy who had so much pull with such important people: at a school like Harrison Central, the lady who runs the cafeteria is as important as anyone in town.

Van's first three years at Harrison Central weren't easy. He had some great teams and again came close to winning the state title, but failed to win the top prize. 1976 was particularly tough because he had state-championship-caliber teams in both the boy's and girl's programs. In a span of seven days Van lost heartbreakers again with both teams, and his season ended abruptly for the second time in three years.

In the boy's district tournament on a Friday, Harrison Central led Biloxi by four with less than two minutes remaining and lost. On the following Thursday, the girl's team, which Van thought was one of the best high school teams he'd ever coached, lost in the state tournament because a number of the team's starters were ill with flu. That spring break was one of the toughest he'd ever had. He'd been in Mississippi high school coaching for twelve years and he'd been close on several occasions, but just couldn't seem to win that final game of the season. He began to doubt himself as a coach again and began to think that it might be his coaching that kept his teams from winning state titles.

But in 1977 it all began to change for Van. Harrison Central started winning—winning big and winning it all. In his final two years at Harrison Central, the Red Rebels were a Mississippi powerhouse in girl's basketball. Van's five-year record at Harrison Central was 227-62 (121-38 boys, 156-24 girls), but in '77 he got his first state title as the girl's team won the State AA championship and finished the season with a mark of 41-3. When the Rebelettes were walking off the court after winning their first state title, Van leaned over to his assistant, Sissy Davis, and said, "Sissy, it just doesn't get any bigger or better than this."

The 1977 girl's team was solid and a state championship was the ultimate goal, but they weren't done there. The Mississippi State High School Athletic Association had an Overall State Championship where the winners of the four classes played each other to determine an overall state champion. Harrison Central won the Overall and Van's team was clearly the best girl's basketball team in the state of Mississippi. After they won the Overall, Van went home to Betty and told her, "This is why I coach. This is everything. This is the ultimate."

"That was the best spring of my life," Van said after winning his first state tournament. "To realize that we won the state championship and had won the last game of the year for the first time in my career was the best feeling in the world. I was on the complete opposite end of the spectrum from a year earlier."

The following year Van lost four starters to graduation from the girl's championship team and nobody gave the team much of a chance of defending their state title. The doubters were probably right; Harrison Central really didn't have much of a chance, but Van made a daring and unprecedented move during the off-season. He invited a gangly freshman named Eugenia Conner to the varsity squad. That move paid off as Conner led Harrison Central to another State AA Championship and another Overall state title.

During their first championship run in 1977, Van was focused on his girl's team and their drive toward a championship. He didn't see any of the junior varsity or middle school games that year, which is a bad move when you're coaching high school basketball. Sooner or later the talent you have moves on to college, and if you haven't been watching the younger players in your school you're in a tough situation at the start of the next season because you don't know what kind of hand you've been dealt. But during the summer following his first title, Van had a number of people in Lyman talking to him about this up-and-coming eighth-grader from North Gulfport Middle School.

Van knew that if he put a ninth-grader on the varsity squad, he would, at the very least, ruffle the feathers of some of the team's seniors and, of course, their parents. So Van spent the entire summer vacation of 1977 worrying about the future of his program, about defending the state title, and about what he was going to do with Eugenia.

He knew she could help Harrison Central, but it was tough to imagine how much advice Van was getting from people all around Lyman. He wasn't necessarily looking for their advice, but he was getting it. Despite how good she was, they all thought that if Van brought her up to the varsity squad it would disrupt the team, the town and the parents. Many of them couldn't understand why Van would even consider it after winning the State AA title a year earlier. Why would he stick his neck out for some fifteen-year-old kid?

He'd made some coaching moves in his life prior to this point and it was all for one thing: W's. He wanted to win more than anything else, and he knew they didn't have a shot unless he at least looked at Eugenia with his other players on the court. He was confident in his decision, knowing that even if it didn't work out, his stock was high enough after winning a state title that he could certainly find another job if things went badly.

At their first practice in the fall of 1977 Van made a deal with his players. He called everyone together to tell them that Eugenia would practice with the varsity team for two weeks; then they would make the decision together. Everyone agreed—not that they had a choice. Van's always said that he has two rules in coaching: 1. The coach is always right, and 2. When the coach is wrong, go back to rule #1.

The toughest decision that he and his coaching staff had to make regarding the Eugenia situation was where to let her dress for practice. The varsity locker room was extremely nice, with carpet, couches, the works. It wasn't a bad setup for a girl's high school basketball team in the late 1970s. The freshman dressing area was a basic locker room—what you would expect. Van didn't know where to put Eugenia for that first practice.

But it didn't take him long to figure out where she would go for the rest of the year. At the first practice in August, the team's starting center stopped at the free-throw line for a jump shot. Eugenia swatted the ball to the half-court line, picked it up, drove the length of the floor and scored. Van turned to Sissy and told her to let Eugenia dress wherever she wanted. He called the team together and said, "I hate to say this, but I don't need two weeks. This is going to make some of you mad, but Eugenia's a member of this team."

Van stuck his neck way out there, but it worked. Again, Harrison Central went 41-3 in the regular season and again won the State AA Championship and the Overall state title—this time with a six-foot-two-inch freshman leading the way.

The 1977–78 championship season was Van's last in high school coaching, though he never would have guessed it. Van was convinced his destiny was to be a high school girl's basketball coach in Mississippi for the remainder of his career. During his high school coaching career, Van was passed over for a lot of college coaching positions. In 1972, he was certain he had the men's head-coaching position at Northwest Junior College, in Senatobia, Mississippi, and a few years later he interviewed for the women's head-coaching positions at Mississippi University for Women and at Mississippi College. Van thought he had them all, but finished no better than second in every instance. He was convinced that, without being a graduate assistant at a college as a young man or knowing certain people in the college ranks, he had been pigeonholed as a high school coach. He even wrote several letters to Bob Weltlich, the men's head coach at Ole Miss, but again nothing.

Despite all the missed opportunities, Van couldn't have been happier during the summer of 1978. He was the head coach of a back-to-back state championship team; he'd broken the $10 thousand per year salary barrier, and was looking forward to another season at Harrison Central where they'd try for three in a row. As a freshman, Eugenia helped lead Harrison Central to a state championship, and Van knew she was just going to get stronger as her high school career continued over the next three years. Things looked good for him at Harrison Central.

❖

During Spring Break 1978, Van drove Betty and their two children, Johnny and Renee, from Lyman on the Mississippi Gulf Coast, four hours to Louisville to visit their parents. At that time Van's dad was still working from sunup to sundown in the cotton fields, and didn't often take a break—no matter who was in town visiting. It upset Van that his father couldn't take a break from his farm to see Betty and his grandchildren, so he left.

Van loaded up the family car after a short visit and headed back to Lyman. The entire time driving he wondered what was going on back in Louisville. It upset his mother that they'd left and he wondered what his dad would say. As they drove up to their house in Lyman, Van could hear the phone ringing from the driveway.

"Son, we got problems," his dad said from the other end of the line. "I've come in here and found out that you've gone home and your mama is so mad she can't see straight. She told me there would be no more sleepin' in the bed with her and I'm in big trouble. You gotta come back up here."

Van smiled, because he knew he had him. It was one of the few times in his life that Van ever heard his dad admit that he was wrong. Van knew he could get his dad out of trouble if they got in the car and headed back, but the very last thing he wanted to do was load up the family and head back to Louisville just so he could get his dad out of hot water.

But again God intervened in Van's life. They hadn't been home thirty minutes when the phone rang again. Van was sure it was his dad begging for them to get in the car, but it was the athletic director at Ole Miss, Warner Alford, wanting to talk to Van about the women's head-coaching position with the Lady Rebels. Although he'd been fighting to get into college coaching for many years, Van surprisingly told Warner that he wasn't interested. In his mind he was set to finish his career as a high school coach in the state in which he grew up; besides, he didn't think the Ole Miss job was that great a position.

Lord knows Betty has saved Van more than once with a good idea, but this was one of her better ones: she had Van ask Warner if the school would pay for their way up to Oxford for the interview. He immediately told Van that they would pay all expenses, and the plan to kill two birds with one stone was in play. Louisville, where the disgruntled grandparents were sitting, was directly between Lyman and Oxford. Van and the family jumped back in the car, drove to Louisville, handed off the kids to the grandparents, and made their way up to Oxford. They didn't take many trips during that time in their lives, and having someone else pay the way made it a small vacation to Oxford.

When they stopped in Louisville to drop off Johnny and Renee, Van told his dad about the call from Warner and the possibility of the Ole Miss job. Winston told him that women's basketball wasn't going anywhere and that he should ask for $20 thousand so he could get as much money as he could while it still lasted. He thought that asking for that obscene amount would scare them off. "Ask for the money, then come home, go back to high school coaching and get happy," was Winston's advice to Van regarding the Ole Miss interview.

As Van and Betty made their way to Oxford and onto the campus of the University of Mississippi, Van didn't particularly want the job. But it didn't take long into the interview with Warner before he realized this wasn't the worst situation he could be in. It was looking better all the time. Van asked Warner where he would have to teach and what subjects he'd be teaching. Warner replied with a laugh, "Hey man, this is the SEC, you don't have to teach." Van then asked Warner about when he would be responsible for cleaning out the gymnasium and sweeping the floors. Van nearly sealed the deal in the wrong direction as Warner busted out laughing.

"Let me tell ya boy, this is big-time college basketball," Warner said with an even bigger laugh. "All you have to do is walk out the door after practice. You don't have to clean up nothin'. Now what's it gonna take to get you here?"

Van said "$18,600," dropping $1400 from his original thoughts. Warner told him later that he was willing to go as high as $23,000, but coming from a $10,000 per year job where he had to clean up the gym every day and teach math courses, $18,600 was all the money in the world.

"I went to Oxford that day and found out that I didn't have to teach and thought I'd died and gone to heaven," Van said. "I wouldn't have minded it though. Teaching classes and picking up dirty towels was still light-years ahead of working in those cotton fields as a kid."

When Van got back to Louisville, his parents were as happy as could be because they'd spent the day with Johnny and Renee, and the kids were twice as happy after spending the day with their grandparents. Van had just gotten an $8,600 raise to move to a college coaching position where all he had to do was coach. That was definitely a memorable day for the Chancellor family.

Van had created a name for himself in Mississippi. From a twenty-one-year-old nobody in Noxapater, to a thirty-three-year-old back-to-back state champion at Harrison Central, people now knew who Van Chancellor was. And it didn't go unnoticed at Ole Miss.

He was on his way. His high school coaching career had taken him from one extreme part of the state to the other, from the Tennessee border to the shores of Mississippi Gulf Coast and it had given him many unforgettable memories. He was ready, ready for big-time college basketball and the Southeastern Conference. He was ready to do it the Lady Rebel Way.

In 1978, women's basketball didn't get any bigger than the Southeastern Conference. I was grateful to be a part of it and I couldn't wait to start coaching in the most competitive league in the country.

Chapter 4
The Lady Rebel Way

IN HIS FIRST SEASON AT Ole Miss, Van was the definition of a lost country boy. He fast learned that coaching on the high school level was a gigantic leap from heading up a college basketball program. In his previous thirteen years of high school coaching, Van did two things: teach mathematics and coach basketball. At Ole Miss, he had to make some adjustments.

He'd never recruited players, managed a budget, spoken at an alumni function or traveled extensively with a team. He was apprehensive, to say the least. He felt comfortable coaching, but all the responsibilities he had away from the basketball court were distracting. During his first two years at Ole Miss he wondered if he'd made the right decision in leaving Harrison Central. He wasn't sure if he could get it done on the college level and the adjustments that he had to make worried him.

His 'to do' list at Ole Miss had a life of its own. He hadn't had any such list on the high school level: at Harrison Central his list had consisted of a rubber band around his wrist so he wouldn't forget to pick up something at the grocery store on the way home. But at Ole Miss he had to break down and start getting organized and his list of things to do began to overwhelm him.

Where am I going to recruit? Who am I going to sign? Who do I call to help me get players? What function am I going to speak at? What do I budget for traveling expenses? What flight are we going to take on the upcoming road trip? What bus service do we use? These are common questions that coaches face today, but it was all new to Van in 1978. The unanswered questions, along with the added pressure of trying to win basketball games in one of the toughest conferences in the country, hung over Van's head.

He left Harrison Central on a high note. Many times in his early days at Ole Miss he longed for the comfort he had at Harrison Central. They had won two straight state titles, and behind Eugenia Conner, Harrison Central went on to win three more consecutive championships after he left for Ole Miss. If Van had stayed at Harrison Central he could easily have been the head coach for five consecutive state championship teams, and it's tough to imagine that record would have ever been broken in Mississippi high school athletics.

Van started at Ole Miss on July 1, 1978. Despite being overwhelmed with emotion over leaving Harrison Central, he was fired up to start his career in the mighty SEC. When he started, his coaching staff consisted of one: himself. However, just before the start of the season, Warner Alford walked into Van's office and introduced him to Rick Walker, a graduate assistant who was hired to assist Van during his first season. Rick was definitely a surprise because Van had no idea he was getting any help from a graduate assistant. Even with Rick by his side during the first year, it was still a nightmare for Van to prepare for the upcoming season. Besides, by the time Rick got there Van had almost everything done; the practice schedule, who would be the starting point guard and what the team was going to eat on the road had already been decided.

But Van was a bit relieved when Rick arrived because he

needed help with the proper etiquette when they were on the road. Van is the first to admit that his etiquette isn't entirely polished. During his thirteen-year career in high school coaching, he hadn't left the Mississippi state line but a handful of times and he never took his team on a road trip that included air travel. At Ole Miss, all Van knew about traveling with the Lady Rebels was that they'd be gone a lot and that he had absolutely no idea how to travel a basketball team across country.

On one of their first road trips in 1978, the team traveled to Miami to play both Penn State and Delta State in the Orange Bowl Classic. When they arrived at the airport in Miami, they had about ninety bags arrive in the baggage claim area. Van and Rick left the bags for the skycap to deliver from the terminal to the team bus waiting outside. While the skycap was loading the bus, the two coaches looked at each other with blank looks on their faces. They knew they had to tip the guy but they were both clueless as to how much. Van reached in his pocket and confidently handed the man a five-dollar bill.

"No puedo hacerlo por ese precio" (I can't do it for that price), screamed the skycap with a scowl on his face. Van's Spanish is limited, that is to say absolutely nonexistent, but he could tell by the skycap's voice that five bucks weren't going to cut it. To Van, there's the English language and then there's the foreign language. That's it—only two languages on the planet. At our first pre-season game in 1997 with the Comets, we had two international players on our team: Janeth Arcain, from Brazil, spoke Portuguese, and Catarina Pollini, from Italy, spoke Italian and was somewhat fluent in English. Following the game against the Sting, Van was upset with Arcain's play earlier in the night and he was trying to make a point outside of Champp's Restaurant after the team had finished eating. "I'm not mad at ya, Janeth. I just need you to rebound the basketball. Rebound the basketball," he

said jumping up and down with his hands in the air. Janeth understood somewhat, but still had a dazed look on her face trying to understand his deep southern drawl. "Catarina, tell her what I said," Van yelled to Pollini, assuming she could speak Janeth's language because, after all, it wasn't English.

After the skycap yelled at Van and Rick over the five-dollar tip, Van reached in his pocket and grabbed a ten-dollar bill and handed it to the skycap attendant, praying that it would satisfy him. *"Estas loco, de niguna manera lo hago!"* (You're crazy, there's no way I can do it!) The skycap was insulted and threw the fifteen dollars to the ground and stormed off. Another Skycap, who'd been watching everything, yelled from across the street, "Hey country boys, the man's looking for fifty cents a bag!" Everyone outside the terminal busted out laughing and Van bent to the ground to pick up the money the skycap left behind. On future road trips, to solve the problem, Van told all his players to carry their own bags from the terminal to the bus. The rule lasted for nineteen years at Ole Miss.

With as many things going on off the court during his first year at Ole Miss, his team's record didn't suffer in his inaugural season at Ole Miss. Van guided the Lady Rebels to a 31-9 mark in the 1978–79 season—the sixth-best during his tenure in Oxford. No one's ever accused Van of being unable to coach, and he's always had the ability to take the talent he's had to put together an adequate team no matter what the circumstances off the court.

But the records took a considerable hit over the next two seasons after the 31-9 inaugural campaign with the Lady Rebels. The only thing he wanted to do at Ole Miss was coach. He didn't want the added responsibilities of heading up an entire program. He was a coach, not an administrator. Give him a whistle, a blackboard and ten athletes willing to give him everything they have, and Van is comfort-able. It's the same in Houston now. Van's title is head coach and general manager of the Houston Comets but he'd rather just coach. It's his love, his passion—it always has been.

Rick Walker left after his first season in 1978–79, and Van's assistant from Harrison Central, Sissy Davis, joined him for the next two years. But there were many sleepless nights and many days spent in an office at the Ole Miss athletic facility when he wondered where his career would be if he'd stayed with Davis back at Harrison Central. Van's never been able to move into a new situation easily. The move to Ole Miss was extremely hard as Van missed the success of Harrison Central. It normally takes Van a few years to get comfortable when he makes a move and he's rarely made a career move without second-guessing him-self.

The 1979–80 Lady Rebels, who finished 23-14, were led by senior Peggie Gillom, who later became Van's assistant at Ole Miss and with the Comets. The team also featured Carol Ross, who is now the head women's basketball coach at the University of Florida. Peggie had an amazing career at Ole Miss, and in March of 1998 she became only the seventh woman ever to be inducted into the Mississippi Sports Hall of Fame. She finished her four years at Ole Miss as the all-time leading scorer (2,486) and rebounder (1,271). Following her senior year she signed with the Dallas Diamonds of the Women's Basketball League, and played with current Detroit Shock head coach Nancy Lieberman-Cline. The WBL was a short-lived, women's professional basketball league in the early 1980s. When Peggie left after graduation, the wins at Ole Miss followed her right out the door.

Van was left scratching his head. In his first two seasons at Ole Miss, the team's combined record was 54-23. But Van wasn't happy and he was having trouble heading up a college basketball program, and now he had to prepare for the 1980–81 season having just lost one of the greatest players he'd ever coached.

He feared the 1980–81 season would be tough, and he was right. That team finished 14-12, the worst finish in his nineteen seasons in Oxford. It was also the only year from 1978 to 1998 that he didn't have Peggie with him, either on the playing floor or by his side on the bench as his assistant. She was in Dallas playing professionally, and the Lady Rebel program struggled without her. When she accepted the head-coaching position at Texas A & M in 1998, Van was incredibly happy for her, but he missed her tremendously. In her final game in Houston, Van grabbed the public address microphone after the game and fought back the tears as he said good-bye and thanked Peggie publicly for all she'd done for him and for everything she meant to his family.

But injuries also played a role in the decline of the Lady Rebel program during the third season. Ole Miss had a significant number of injuries; everyone on the team missed at least one game due to injury except for Ross. The starting five never were together during the entire twenty-six-game schedule. In his thirty-four years of coaching, Van's never had an injury-filled season like the 1980–81 fiasco at Ole Miss. The Lady Rebels could have easily asked for combat pay after that grisly season.

❖

Van knew the program was in trouble and he knew he needed help. Fortunately he got some following the third season. But the biggest turnaround came from within. Van promised himself that he was going to work as hard as he's ever worked preparing for the 1981–82 season and that he was going to give it one more year. If he couldn't get the Lady Rebel program turned around during the fourth season, then he knew it was time to get out. But what fired Van up more than anything else following the 1980–81 season was what he heard through the grapevine back at Harrison Central. One of his close friends, or former close friends, was telling people in Lyman that "If Chancellor doesn't get that thing turned around at Ole Miss, they're gonna get rid of him." Van's always been about loyalty, and that statement made him so mad, so determined to win, that he wasn't going to quit now for anything.

There's no doubt that he got some breaks heading into that fourth year. He was more fired up now than ever before about getting the thing turned around, and he got some outside help as well. Peggie played just one season in the WBL, and returned to Oxford when Van asked her to be his assistant. That was probably the smartest move in his coaching career. Peggie and Van were a great team and the 1981–82 season was the start of a great coaching duo.

Sissy, Van's assistant for the previous two seasons, left Ole Miss after the dismal third season, electing to return to high school coaching. Ironically, she became the head girl's basketball coach at Winston Academy High School in Van's hometown of Louisville. The Ole Miss coaching staff was nearly complete for the 1981–82 campaign, which included Van in seat one and Peggie in seat two. But before Peggie ever accepted the job at Ole Miss, Warner Alford told Van he had more money for additional help if he needed it. That's the beauty about being close with an athletic director on the college level—there's always a little extra money laying around if one of your coaches really needs it. Van needed it.

He got his money's worth out of Joe Corley. Corley was hired to help Van and Peggie turn things around at Ole Miss and help them with their recruiting efforts. It turned out to be one of the major reasons for the Lady Rebel turn-around following the 14-12 season in 1980–81.

Corley absolutely drove Van nuts. He called him almost every morning, dragged his butt out of bed and, by the time

Van got to his office, Corley had the entire day's agenda laid out on his desk. He had Van going from sunup to sundown, but he helped him get his foot in the door on more than one occasion while recruiting players. He had lists of people for Van to call, and if Van didn't feel like making a recruiting trip, Corley was in his ear making sure it happened. He lived with Van for the first two weeks he was in Oxford and he always had a game plan each day, whether Van liked it or not.

"If you want to sign this player, coach, then I think you ought to be here," he would continually tell Van. One night during the spring of 1981, Corley found out that Rochelle Thompson, one of the top recruits during that time, was in Oxford. Corley called Van and told him that they had to go visit her. It was late, about 11:00 P.M., and Van didn't feel like disturbing her or the friends she was visiting. But they made the trip, talked with Rochelle, and had her on the roster that fall.

Corley's high energy level was simply driving Van crazy, but he knew he needed the help. Corley had Van at all the right places in every corner of Mississippi. Corley had no other interests except making Ole Miss a winner.

❖

Van had recruited a lot of good players for the start of the 1981–82 season and he felt a lot better about his team's chances with Peggie by his side again. But there was still one unsigned national top recruit, who just happened to reside in Mississippi. She was ranked the top high school player in the country, and every school from California to New York wanted her, including Van in tiny Oxford, Mississippi. The Ole Miss coaching staff worked feverishly each day to try to sign her because they knew she would immediately make the program not only better but one of the toughest in the nation. She didn't sign at the end of her senior year of high school. She chose, instead, to spend time at home with friends and family during the summer vacation. In fact, she didn't sign in May, June or July. Peggie started her new position at Ole Miss in the first week of July 1981, and her first assignment was to find a way to sign this top recruit.

It should have been an easy recruit for Van because he hated to see a player from Mississippi leave to play somewhere else. He always put his best effort toward a Mississippi player, and besides, this player was one of the top recruits in the nation and they went after her hard. She was living in Gulfport, and Ole Miss wanted her to stay home and play, so it should have been a slam-dunk for Van and Peggie. It wasn't.

Eugenia Conner, the player Van coached at Harrison Central during her freshman year in high school and who led the Lady Rebels to four consecutive State AA titles, was easily the most recognizable African American female athlete in the country and the one everyone was after. Eugenia wanted to stay home, but under no circumstances was she going to play for a school that prided itself in waving and displaying the Confederate flag. Even when she was a senior in high school she told everyone that she would love to play for Van at Ole Miss, but she just couldn't play under a flag that she felt stood for hatred and racism.

Van fought the Confederate flag for nineteen seasons at Ole Miss. He and Peggie never went on a recruiting trip to an African American home where they didn't have to explain the flag's heritage. When Van arrived at Ole Miss in 1978, Peggie was the only African American player on the team. They lost a lot of recruits over the years because of the flag issue at Ole Miss. But Peggie always felt that if they could get the player to Oxford and to the Ole Miss campus, they would have a shot at signing them. It's no surprise; you can't be around Peggie for very long and not feel at home. Peggie definitely made African American recruits feel welcome, and there's no telling how many recruits they would have lost if Peggie hadn't have been by Van's side. African American athletes didn't want to play at Ole Miss; many still don't, and Van and Peggie had to fight it every year.

But Van wanted to win and he knew they had to fight through this flag issue. With Eugenia on the court, not only would Ole Miss start to win, they'd become a national power overnight. Van met with Peggie and Joe Corley every day during July, trying to figure out a way to sign her. Her talent on the court was obvious, but signing Eugenia would open a lot of recruiting doors for years to come. Van knew that if they could sign her, many other talented African American players wouldn't be so hesitant in signing with Ole Miss in the future.

Peggie finally went to Van one day in early August and said, "Coach, I'm just tired of it. We ain't gonna sign her. Let's just give up on it and concentrate on what we do have."

"Peggie, give it one more day," he said. "Give me one more day's effort."

One of Peggie's friends at the school was Lucius Williams, an African American administrator at Ole Miss. She hoped he'd have an idea, or might know someone who could help them sign Eugenia. Williams knew Carolyn Henderson, an attorney in Gulfport, Eugenia's hometown. Carolyn received her law degree from Ole Miss and had always wanted to repay the school in some way. It was a start, and Van and Peggie started digging to see if they could make a connection between Carolyn Henderson and Eugenia Conner. It didn't take long before they discovered that Henderson was the attorney for Eugenia's mother, Shirley. It was a small opening, and Van and Peggie blew it wide open.

Peggie got her on the phone, and then handed it to Van, who laid it on pretty heavy for Carolyn. Van did all he could to get her excited about Ole Miss, Eugenia and college basketball. By the end of the conversation he had her so fired up about the possibilities for her client's daughter that she couldn't wait to get off the phone and call Shirley Conner.

"All right, Van. I'm excited. You got me. What do you want me to do?" she asked.

"I got one month, and we can go big time with Eugenia," Van told her in an excited voice. "Let's get down to the bottom line. If in the next month you become a really good lawyer, we won't sign Eugenia. But if you become an average lawyer and a real good recruiter for Ole Miss, we're gonna sign the girl and be a national power." Henderson loved Ole Miss and this really got her going.

Finally, after months of work and endless hours of conversation with Carolyn Henderson, Ole Miss signed Eugenia just five days before school started. Just before joining the Ole Miss staff, Peggie purchased a new car from the money she earned while playing professionally in Dallas. By the end of the first season at Ole Miss, the car had 53,000 miles on it—a majority of them from traveling back and forth from Oxford to Gulfport while talking with Eugenia. Van and Peggie had taken a huge step in building a nationally ranked program when they signed Eugenia, and, in the meantime, took a shot at the flag that had hurt Ole Miss recruiting for so many years.

❖

Fortunately for Van, Warner Alford let him grow into the Ole Miss job. It took Van those first three years to get comfortable as a college coach. Not that anyone at the school was complaining. Even while Van was finding his comfort zone from 1978–1981, he led the Lady Rebels to an overall record of 68-35. It was obvious he could coach on the college level; he just needed to find a comfort zone. Everything began to fall into place in the summer of 1981. He had Joe Corley driving him all over Mississippi recruiting players, he had Peggie back by his side and he and Betty began to establish a network of friends in Oxford. The St. Andrew's Methodist Church helped guide the way for the two. The church softball team became nearly a daily event for the Chancellors, and the fellowship they received started to put Van at ease.

Now that he was comfortable, understood his responsibilities off the court, had Peggie back on the sidelines and Eugenia on the court, the Lady Rebel program took off. During Eugenia's four years at Ole Miss, the Lady Rebels went 106-20, including a trip to the NCAA regional finals where they came just one game short of the 1985 Final Four.

The 1985 team was arguably one of Van's best ever. Eugenia was a senior and the team finished 29-3 overall and won 24 straight at one point in the middle of the season. Unfortunately, a season that opened with such excitement also brought unwelcome sorrow into the Chancellor home. The team traveled to Honolulu in early January where they destroyed Abilene Christian, Temple, and Hawaii to improve to 11-1 on the year. When they returned to Mississippi, Betty's grandmother, who had been in a coma for several years, finally died from complications. It was the first of many setbacks to come that year.

With the family loss behind them, the Lady Rebels picked up where they left off and continued to roll through the season. Van had a lot of fun with that team because he knew they were good and he knew they had a chance of winning every time they took the floor—every time. They won their next sixteen straight, and were ranked as high as number three in the country. Van's parents made the two-hour drive from Louisville to Oxford for all the weekend games. On Feb. 3, 1985, Van's father and a friend made the trek to Ole Miss to see the Lady Rebels dispose of Kentucky 82-56 on a Saturday afternoon. Van's mother didn't make the trip, however, which concerned him because she was always the instigator for the trips to Oxford. She loved Ole Miss women's basketball and was Van's biggest fan. She suffered from severe arthritis, and Van thought that was the reason why she didn't make the trip to Oxford.

The next day Van called home to Louisville to check on his mom. Van's never been the kind of guy to get on the phone and gush over emotions, but on that particular day he called his mother to check on her health and specifically to tell her that he loved her. At that time the Chancellor family didn't know if she was seriously ill or just fighting a weekend illness. But just three days later she was rushed to the emergency room in Louisville, where doctors discovered lung cancer.

Van was not aware of the emergency room visit as he was preparing for a game against Memphis State later that night. Following the game, Van's dad dropped the bomb on him, telling him that hours earlier his mother had been diagnosed with cancer. However, the word of the cancer didn't strike the fear into him as it would most of us, since his father had undergone successful surgery for lung cancer in 1977. Both of his parents were heavy smokers, and Van held fast to the idea that his mom would have surgery and recover just as his father had eight years earlier.

Van still felt that he should head back to Louisville after he got the news from his dad. Mississippi had been hit by a hard freeze earlier in the day, but Van still wanted to try it. Mel Chrestman, the Lady Rebels' play-by-play announcer, offered Van and Betty his four-wheel drive truck for the trip to Louisville, and the two crept along the frozen highway at an extremely slow pace. A trip that normally took two hours took nearly four that night in what was clearly one of the longest trips of Van's life.

They arrived at the Louisville hospital at 2:30 A.M. Van's father, brother and grandmother met them in the waiting room. But when Van walked in the front door, he realized that it was going to take more than routine surgery to save his mother. Van's family had long faces as they delivered the news that his mother was in critical condition with lung cancer and cancer of the uterus. The doctor told the family that the best they could do now was to make her comfortable—words that tore Van apart.

The news shook Van and the entire family as well. Van's mom was the oldest of six children. When her father died when she was ten years old, she helped her mother raise her brothers and sisters. She was a very gracious and loving person and the entire extended family depended upon her. On February 11, just seven days after Van found out that his mom was sick, she died of lung cancer.

Talk to Van about his mother and it doesn't take long to figure out that he was certainly a mama's boy. His mom loved basketball and if there had been a Van Chancellor Fan Club during his tenure at Ole Miss, she would have been the self-appointed president. She took a real interest in the game and in Van's coaching abilities. One night, following a win at Horn Lake, Van was feeling rather good about himself but his mother was silent in the car on the way home. "Mama, pretty big win, huh? What do you think about the way I coached tonight?" he asked. She said, "Boy, I thought you'd never ask," as she reached into her purse and pulled out her grocery list pad and proceeded to read off five ways she thought Van should have coached the game differently.

Her death took Van's breath away because no one in the family was expecting it and it happened so incredibly quickly. It's not often in today's world that you see a grown man cry when he talks about his mother, but he still does it to this day. She was a huge support in his life, and now she was gone, right in the middle of a season he knew she would have enjoyed. Van's ties with his family have been strong since the time he could crawl, and family is still the most important thing in his life. The death of his mom during the most successful year in his career had an effect on him the remainder of the season. Ole Miss was clearly a favorite to contend for the NCAA title in 1985 but their chances took a serious jolt when his mom passed away.

At the time of her death, Ole Miss was 22-1; easily one of the top teams in the nation and a favorite to reach the Final Four. They won their last four games following his mom's death and finished the regular season at 26-1. On February 13, just two days after Van's mom died, they barely beat Auburn 66-65. A day earlier, the Ole Miss team bus was waiting for him following the funeral and he jumped in and sat through one of the longest bus rides of his life as they headed down the highway toward Auburn. Van was very close to the players from the 1985 team and they respected his feelings and privacy the entire trip. He spoke briefly to Betty on a 4½-hour trip that felt like 104½. Playing the game against Auburn is what his mother would have wanted, and it helped him get his mind off the last several hours. The game ended up being therapeutic for him—nothing more.

❖

Ole Miss entered the SEC tournament in 1985 as the number one seed in the Western Division. They defeated Mississippi State 88-45 in the first round but were defeated by Tennessee in the semifinal round 79-71 on March 2, 1985—the team's first loss since Dec. 3, 1994. The Lady Rebels were still a high seed in the NCAA tournament. They defeated Southern Mississippi 81-68 in the first round and got revenge on Tennessee in the Mideast regional semifinals by defeating the Lady Vols 63-60. The legendary Pat Summitt, who had also coached the United States Olympic team in 1984, was the head coach at Tennessee. Before the game, Van shook hands with the officials and asked if they were going to have the guts to stand up to the Olympic coach and make the tough calls. Pat later told Van that she thought that was the reason Ole Miss won the game. For forty minutes the officials did everything they could to prove they could stand up to her and weren't afraid of her. Whatever it takes—Van likes to win.

With the wins over Southern Miss and Tennessee, Van was now just one win away from taking Ole Miss to the Final Four in Austin, Texas. But before they could schedule their little Final Four trip they had to get by Western Kentucky in the regional final game played on the Western Kentucky campus. Western Kentucky was on a high because the night before, they defeated Texas in the other regional semifinal game. Texas was the top seed in the Mideast regional, and the clear favorite to reach the Final Four. There's no doubt that Western Kentucky's win over the Longhorns had them pumped and they were just waiting for Ole Miss on their home floor.

The game against Western Kentucky was Van's first crack at a Final Four appearance and a possible national championship, but his head just wasn't in it. He had a heavy heart that night in Kentucky, as the recent death of his mom still gripped his emotions. He had been getting by on fragile emotions ever since his mother's death because there had never been a chance to grieve. He was physically and emotionally drained. Throughout the entire forty minutes, he kept thinking about her, not only about how proud she would have been, but also how much fun she would be having at this great game. Ole Miss lost 72-68 in a heartbreaker, and the season that opened with such promise and excitement, ended with despair, depression and heartache.

"I don't feel like I did a bad job of coaching, but I just don't think I was razor-sharp," he said of his effort against Western Kentucky. "I was a mama's boy. Losing my mother was the biggest shock of my life. I coached that team to the regional finals, but I just never did regain my spirit that year."

But as much as Van thought he wasn't razor-sharp that night, neither was his team. It was just one of those games when a team couldn't get anything started. Ole Miss had two of the best players in school history on the floor and both struggled. Jennifer Gillom, Peggie's little sister, who Van recruited in 1983 and is now a member of the WNBA's Phoenix Mercury, and Eugenia shot a combined 9-for-25 from the field, and Eugenia finished with just seven points, well under her four-year career average of sixteen points per game.

❖

In his first seven seasons at Ole Miss, the four from 1981–85 with Peggie on the bench and Eugenia on the court were his most successful and most memorable. The wins kept coming, and along with them the recruits followed. Jennifer Gillom was one of the biggest recruits to come to Ole Miss during Eugenia's era. She and Eugenia were teammates for three seasons from 1982–85 and Jennifer was the inside force for Ole Miss her senior year after Eugenia graduated.

Van and Eugenia built a special bond over those four years. He gambled on her in 1977 and brought her up as a freshman to play on the Harrison Central varsity squad. He fought every day after she graduated from Harrison Central to convince her to join him at Ole Miss. Their friendship grew from there and became stronger during their four years together in Oxford. When she completed her social work degree from Ole Miss in 1985, she headed to Italy to play professionally. Before the WNBA, gifted women's basketball players were forced to continue their careers overseas. Eugenia spent four seasons away from her family before hanging up her sneakers in 1990. She headed back to Gulfport and worked in the Mississippi Department of Human Services for four years. Shortly thereafter, in March 1994, Eugenia died of a massive heart attack due to a hyperactive thyroid. Mississippi had lost a great athlete, children in Gulfport lost a fierce advocate in the Department of Human Services, and Van had lost a close friend all too soon.

The announcement of Eugenia's death was another major blow. Although this shocker hit him nearly ten years after his mom's death, Van knew how much Eugenia had helped mold his career in the early years at Ole Miss. One of his closest friends, a woman who'd done so much for his career, had died suddenly at the age of thirty and he simply couldn't believe it. He felt so bad for her family and the community of Gulfport because she was such a role model to everyone in the area.

He was asked to speak at her funeral at the Harrison Central High School gymnasium, where the two had so many memories together. He struggled that day, from the time they got in the car until after he was back home from the funeral. He was so filled with emotion when he walked into the Harrison Central gymnasium that he couldn't stop crying. He was back in the gym where he and Eugenia had had so much success in high school, and he couldn't stop reliving all the great times they'd shared.

He knew that she had made his career, and getting up speaking in front of the crowd that had gathered was one of the toughest things he'd ever had to do. Eugenia gave such hope to everyone, and had been incredibly unselfish in giving up basketball in Italy to return home and help the people of Gulfport.

Van began to panic just moments before he had to speak at her funeral. He wasn't sure if he was going to get through it without sobbing uncontrollably. He stood in the back of the gymnasium with Peggie, who was also jolted by the sudden news. Eugenia was Peggie's first recruit at Ole Miss and they, too, had built a special bond.

When he got to the podium he was visibly shaken. His eyes were puffy, his cheeks were red and his heart heavy. "I have a lot of things in my heart that I want to say, but there's no way in the world I can express to you how I feel right now because I cannot keep from crying," he told the audience gathered in the hot, sweaty gym. "I'm going to say a few things and then I'm going to sit down, but I don't want anyone here to think that I don't have a lot of things to say. I just have no way of saying them right now."

Van uses his humor to get him out of tight spots, and he relied on it heavily that day. It was really his only choice because he knew he had no chance of talking about Eugenia unless he made everyone laugh. "Many years ago, when Eugenia was playing for me at Ole Miss, we used to make fun of each other," he said. "I turned to Eugenia on the bus one day before a game and said, 'Eugenia, you're so ugly that when you were little, your mama had to tie a bone around your neck just to get the dog to play with you.' She replied, 'Well, you know coach, I was in English class the other day and our professor asked me to give the definition of *ugly*. I told him to look in the dictionary under Van Chancellor.'"

That brought the house down and Van was able to make his way back to his seat while everyone was laughing. He sat there with a heavy heart, yes, but knowing that Eugenia would have enjoyed that story. He spent the rest of the day reflecting on how much she meant to him and how she impacted his life. Without Eugenia coming to Ole Miss, the 14-12 season in 1981 might have become more than a memory—it might have become the norm.

Eugenia Conner was a very big part of Van's life and of his success on the sidelines. Not only was she one of the greatest players to play at Ole Miss, but she also enabled Van and Peggie to recruit other great African American athletes in and around Mississippi. But of all the things she brought to his life, the greatest was friendship.

The friendship was there long after her career and life were over.

Chapter 5
Fighting for the Final Four

VAN BEGAN HIS COACHING CAREER in 1965 at a tiny high school in Noxapater, Mississippi. His ultimate goal in 1965 was to someday be named the head coach of men's basketball at an NCAA Division I university. In 1985 he thought he'd reached it.

The summer following their magical run in the 1985 NCAA tournament, falling just one game short of the Final Four, Lee Hunt, the men's basketball coach at Ole Miss, resigned his position with the Rebels to become the new men's head coach at the University of Missouri-Kansas City. Van thought he had a shot at the men's job because he was popular with everyone in the Ole Miss athletic department and almost everyone in Oxford. After leading the women's team to the 29-3 mark and a regional final a year earlier, he thought he certainly had the inside track on completing his dream of being named men's coach.

Hunt resigned in August 1985, just weeks before the start of the new school year. Van went to a large alumni function in Jackson after Hunt's resignation, thinking the job was his. The timing couldn't have been better because Ole Miss was forced to find a new men's coach in just a few short weeks before school started, and everyone in the athletic department knew Van and respected him as a coach.

He also felt he had the support of all the players and assistant coaches on the men's team. He had worked hard for seven years as the women's coach at Ole Miss and he was ready to make the jump into SEC men's basketball. However, though he never knew it, Van was never even considered for the job.

Warner interviewed only one candidate: Ed Murphy from Division II Delta State University in Cleveland, Mississippi. A year earlier, Murphy guided Delta State to a win over Mississippi State in Starkville. Any time Mississippi State gets beat in their own place it gets the attention of the Ole Miss faithful. Murphy had a lot of support from influential Ole Miss alumni, and Van didn't solicit any additional alumni support. A few weeks after Hunt resigned, Murphy was named the new coach. Van was crushed.

It hurt, but didn't come as a huge surprise. When Van hadn't been named coach four or five days after Hunt resigned, he realized that the job wasn't his. He thought, "If you're in the house and you don't get invited to the dinner table, you realize you ain't eating."

Although Van's name had been knocked around for the men's position, the university president, Gerald Turner, felt it would better benefit the school to keep Van in the women's position because he'd done a decent job with the program. Warner agreed because, as athletic director, the last thing he wanted to do was disrupt one of his nationally ranked programs, and the women's team was exactly where he wanted it to be.

Turner's decision to keep Van with the women's program initially upset him, but ironically the school president later became a huge Lady Rebel fan and supported them for many years. He came to a lot of games, both home and on the road, and gave Van a lot of financial resources to help him succeed over the years. He didn't give Van the men's job in 1985, but it turned out to be a blessing and one of the biggest favors anyone has ever done for him. He wouldn't be where he is today if he'd been named men's head coach at Ole Miss. But at the time it irked him nonetheless.

After getting the brush from the Ole Miss administration, Van felt that his days as the coach of the Lady Rebels were coming to a close. Because it was so late in the summer, his plan was to stay at Ole Miss for one more season and then look for other work following the 1985–86 season. He was coming off a great season where his team went 29-3, but he still felt his welcome in Oxford had been worn out. For the two weeks following Murphy's hire, Van had the worst attitude in his thirty-four-year coaching career.

He was hurt by the administration at Ole Miss, and sulked following the disappointment of not getting the men's job. But he soon found that the best remedy for the pain was actually becoming a friend with Murphy. He knew it would be easy to become resentful of the man, and most would agree that he had every reason to feel that way. But Van's always said that the people you worry about the most, and the people you resent in this world, are out playing golf and don't care what you're thinking or worrying about. Murphy treated Van with great respect and they began to get very close.

Although Van was bitter at first toward the school, he didn't stay that way for long. His initial thought was to leave Ole Miss, but instead of sulking he tackled the 1985–86 season like no other in his career. It's as if he had something to prove to the Ole Miss administration for making the mistake of not hiring him as their new men's coach. If they wanted him as women's head coach, that's what they were going to get—the best money could buy. Ole Miss fought through the 1985–86 season and had another successful year, going 24-8 and reaching their second NCAA regional final and another chance of going to the Final Four. Once he didn't get the men's job and got over that two-week slump, he put it behind him and started coaching with every ounce of ability he had.

The Lady Rebels had their backs against the wall that season as they lost three starters from the team that had taken them to the regional final a year earlier. Eugenia, who finished her career third on the all-time scoring list at Ole Miss, graduated; the team missed her tremendously. Marilyn Brooks, currently twelfth on the school's all-time scoring list, and Deborah Temple, who led the nation in scoring while she was at Division II Delta State before transferring to Ole Miss, were also lost to graduation. Van thought his team would have a decent year in 1985–86, but 24-8 and another trip to the regional final was way beyond his expectations.

But even without Eugenia, Brooks and Temple, Van had a senior center in Jennifer Gillom who was as good as any player in the Southeastern Conference if not the country. Gillom finished second to her sister in scoring at Ole Miss, at 2,186 points. She was a bruiser—a real force inside and she could score at will, especially during her senior season. She holds Ole Miss school records for most points in a season (742) and scoring average (23.2), both set in 1985–86.

Van also had to rely on junior guard Alisa Scott, who is currently sixth on the Ole Miss all-time scoring list. Scott was named Van's assistant coach with the Comets after Peggie had left for Texas A&M. Although they entered the 1985–86 campaign short-handed, Van certainly had a solid inside-outside combination in Gillom and Scott.

He had to make another adjustment that season because Gillom was the only player that year with any size at six-feet-three-inches. The previous year Van had a potent inside game with Eugenia and Jennifer posting up. When Eugenia left, the majority of the size went with her. Van had to change Ole Miss' philosophy and coaching style to be successful. They changed their style, and they succeeded.

Van sat his coaching staff down at the beginning of training camp and told them that the only way they'd win any games was to not let Jennifer Gillom foul out of any game under any circumstances. Gillom led the SEC in scoring and was easily the team's biggest weapon. She could score from anywhere. Van's never claimed to be the smartest guy on the planet, but he knew at the very least that they needed to have her in the game in order to win. Any time Jennifer's "man" got the ball, there was to be help coming from every other direction. Under no circumstances was Jennifer to attempt a blocked shot during that season.

❖

Prior to the start of the 1985–86 season, the coaching staff also underwent another change as Joe Corley headed back to Taylorsville, Mississippi to run a small restaurant. There was now an opening for an assistant to join Van and Peggie. Being an assistant coach at Ole Miss carried a lot of responsibility because it entailed recruiting responsibilities. And recruiting at Ole Miss, despite Oxford's Southern charm, can sometimes be a handful because of the Rebel flag that flies daily on campus.

Jack Gadd joined the Lady Rebel coaching staff in the summer of 1985. He was an assistant high school coach in Hickory Flat, Mississippi for several years, and he and Van had become friends while Van was at Ole Miss. One Saturday morning in 1983, Jack called and asked to see Van. Van crawled out of bed, didn't shave, put on some ragged clothes and threw on a baseball cap. He thought Jack was having some personal problems and Van was more than willing to lend an ear to a good friend.

But as the conversation with Jack continued, so did the ride in his truck. They finally reached the Student Union on the Ole Miss campus and Jack told Van he wanted him to meet some friends. As Van entered the room he realized it was an Amway meeting and Jack had brought him there to become a salesman. Van looked around and saw everybody else in the place in suits and ties; he was in sweats and a baseball cap and had an unshaven face. He was embarrassed, extremely angry, and ready to go to blows with Jack.

According to Van, as he took a seat, the speaker for the Amway group stood up and said, "If there's anybody in this room who's not interested in making a million dollars, or in owning your own boat, or vacationing in Hawaii, I suggest you leave now." Van got up and left. Jack got up and followed him all the way back to the truck. Van wanted to go home and Jack didn't talk to him the entire trip back to his house.

"Gadd, I'm going to forget this morning, but if you ever, ever mention Amway again to me the rest of my life, I will never speak to you again, *ever*," he said after he got out of the truck and slammed the door shut.

"You mad?" Jack asked.

"Mad? If I wasn't a churchgoing man, I'd give you a butt-whippin' right now for embarrassing me like that," Van said.

Two years later, when Corley resigned, Jack applied for the assistant coaching position. Van thought to himself that anyone who tried to get him to sell Amway was bound to be able to recruit players, so Van hired him and he stayed with Ole Miss for the next two years.

With the coaching staff in place, Ole Miss again had a fairly successful regular season for the second straight year and the Lady Rebels were again one of the powers in the SEC and would certainly get a bid for the NCAA tournament.

Auburn had crushed them by twenty-five points in the last regular-season game of the year, and as they made their way through the NCAA tournament, Auburn loomed in the distance. Both Ole Miss and Auburn kept winning in the NCAA tournament and both teams were on a crash course to meet up again. They did, in the regional semifinals in Austin, Texas.

The mood in the bus on the way to games that season was always lighthearted—not many buses in Van's coaching career have been anything less. He likes to keep things upbeat on the way to games, something he's done his entire career. But on the way to the showdown with Auburn, Van was doing all he could to think of a way to get his team feeling positively as they prepared to play a team that had beaten them by twenty-five the last time they met.

Van stood up and said, "Gang, here's what I think. This baby's going to come down to the last play, a last shot, perhaps a last-second free throw, and somebody's got to step up and make it."

"Hey coach, whatever you do, let me get fouled—you know I'll make it," Jennifer Gillom said.

"No, no, no—you know coach that if it comes down to the wire, *I'm* the player you want at the line. Make sure they foul me, you know I'll make it," Alisa Scott said.

By this time the bus had become full of chatter, as all the players were either busting out laughing or telling each other to sit down. The scenario of a last second free throw had everybody talking.

"You know I can shoot it, coach. Give *me* the ball," said the team's point guard, Kim Bullard, who shot 73 percent from the line over her four-year career.

The last person to jump up and give her two cents was senior Vikki Craig. Craig was a team captain along with Gillom and was a perfect role player while the two were on the floor. Gillom shot the ball every time she touched it, and Craig was a great defender and rebounder. She wasn't on the floor to shoot and she and Van both knew it.

She struggled from the line, shooting just 40 percent for the year.

"You know as well as I do coach that I shouldn't have the ball at the end, right?" Craig said seriously. Van laughed and everybody on the bus reacted. Anyone who knew anything about Ole Miss Lady Rebel basketball knew they weren't going to have Craig shooting down the stretch.

Ole Miss battled Auburn for forty minutes and, unlike the last time they played when Auburn won 81-56, the Lady Rebels stayed close from start to finish. The winner would move on to play Texas, ranked number one and unbeaten on the year, for the right to move onto the Final Four. As Ole Miss fought with Auburn, time finally ran out in regulation and the two teams were tied. Van was right— it was going to go down to the wire.

The game went back and forth in overtime and with it tied and time winding down in the extra period, Auburn held for one last shot for the win before forcing double overtime. As Auburn shot with little time remaining, the ball came off the rim into Vicki Craig's hands and she was fouled with one desperate tick remaining. Ole Miss was in the bonus and Vicki was now faced with a one-and-one opportunity and a chance to send the Lady Rebels to the regional finals for the second straight year.

The irony was incredibly thick that Vicki was actually at the line in overtime for a chance at the win. She was clearly the worst free-throw shooter in the building and they had joked about it just hours earlier in the bus. Van was thinking double overtime as he felt there was absolutely no way she was going to hit a free throw with that much pressure.

But she stepped to the line with her heart in her throat and buried the free throw to give Ole Miss a 56-55 lead with one second remaining. Van jumped off his chair and, amidst the chaos, the sweat, the screaming players and the roaring crowd, told Peggie that he wanted her to intentionally miss the second free throw so time would expire as the ball came off the rim. Peggie grabbed Van and said, "Are you crazy? That's the stupidest idea I've heard all night."

Not very many people in this world can look Van in the eye in such a pressure situation and talk to him like that. In fact there are only two: Betty and Peggie. When Peggie had an idea late in the game, Van was going to listen. She scowled at him and was adamant about not letting her miss the second free throw intentionally.

"Well fine then, Peggie," Van screamed above the noise of the crowd and players. "Give me one good reason why I shouldn't have her miss the second one."

"You're crazy. The girl hasn't made two free throws in a row in her entire life," Peggie screamed. "If you tell her to miss the second one, she'll shoot an air-ball and they'll get it back. You leave her alone up there! Don't say a word to her—I promise she'll miss the second one."

It's tough to talk Van out of something. He'll listen, but it's tough to convince him if he knows he's right. But he went with Peggie on the free throw and looked out to Vicki at the free throw line. "Put it in Vicki, great job, just put this second one in," he yelled as he clapped his hands and gave her a confident nod from the sidelines.

Craig threw up a perfect missed free throw after that. The ball clanked around forever on the rim and Auburn never had a chance to throw up a desperation shot. When she missed it and the buzzer sounded, Van ran onto the court and jumped into Vicki's arms at the free-throw line. An Austin newspaper photographer captured the jubilation and it ran on the front page of the sports section the following day.

Van couldn't believe it. It was like the team looked into a crystal ball on the way to the game and talked about how somebody was going to have to step up and hit a big shot down the stretch to beat Auburn in a tight game. Vicki

Craig's improbable free throw gave Ole Miss the 56-55 win in overtime and another shot at getting to the Final Four as they advanced to the regional finals against Texas. For the second straight year Van was one game short of the Final Four, and again for the second straight year he faced one of the hottest teams in America on their home floor.

❖

Defeating the University of Texas in Austin wasn't going to be an easy task. Actually, defeating the University of Texas anywhere on the planet was an impossible task that year. The Longhorns entered the game with a record of 31-0 and were the top-rated team in the country. Going back to the previous season, the Lady Longhorns were 56-1 over their last fifty-seven games, including a 30-0 mark at home at the Frank Erwin Center on the campus of the University of Texas.

There was a buzz about that game in the circles of women's basketball. Ole Miss was clearly the underdog but Van still felt they had a good enough team and a chance of knocking off mighty Texas. The Longhorns were led by Kamie Ethridge, Beverly Williams and Fran Harris, who later played for Van during the inaugural WNBA season in Houston. Texas simply destroyed teams during the 1985–86 regular season, with an average margin of victory of 27.8 points per game. They also cruised through the post-season in the SWC tournament and the NCAA tournament, winning by a margin of 21.7 points per game.

Texas defeated Oklahoma 85-59 in the regional semifinal the same night Ole Miss got past Auburn in overtime. Obviously Texas was favored, but the Lady Rebels didn't enter the game as pushovers either. They were 24-7 at that point and had beaten a lot of good teams during the regular and post-season as well. Earlier that season, Ole Miss had tangled with Texas in Miami at the Orange Bowl Classic, losing 57-46. The Lady Rebels were ranked number eight in the country at the time, and Van felt good about the way they had played.

Ole Miss had stayed close with Texas most of the game when the two teams hooked up earlier in the season, but they didn't shoot the ball well and didn't play one of their better games. When they got set to play Texas in the regional finals, Van was more worried about playing them at their home stadium than about anything else. He knew that as far as talent was concerned, they could play with them.

Van was a bundle of nerves before the Texas game. Jack Gadd gave Van every reason to believe they had a chance, but he was still nervous and worried about his team's mental attitude. The night before the game, Van and Jack got together to figure out a way to beat the Longhorns. As the night wore on, Jack began to convince Van that they had a shot at winning. Surprisingly, it didn't calm his nerves; instead it made him even more nervous because the thought of actually knocking off Texas was starting to seem obtainable.

Peggie dealt with the situation a little differently: she calmed the team by taking them to a movie in Austin. While they were off enjoying the movie, Van and Jack were back at the hotel convincing each other that they could actually pull this thing off. Van felt prepared going into that game and he felt good when Peggie and the team returned to the hotel. He got the entire team together in his room because he had some thoughts he wanted to run by them. When Van has a thought about a game, it's best just to hear him out.

The team staggered into Van's room in pajamas and robes as he, Peggie, Jack, and Betty were waiting. He could tell they were irritated when they entered, but he was ready to give the most inspirational speech in college basketball history. He was ready to give his players every reason why they were going to defeat Texas the following day. If Van and Jack had stayed in that hotel room long enough they would have solved all the world's problems, too. It was a brainstorming session in the purest sense of the word and by the time they were done, the two coaches thought they could have beaten the Boston Celtics.

After Van was done and the blood was pumping and the emotions flying, he was waiting for a huge roar from his players and coaching staff. Instead he got "Coach, I cannot believe you got me out of bed and drug me down here to tell me something that everybody in this room already knows," Alisa Scott said. "Everybody here knows we're going to beat Texas—now just relax and go to bed." As far as confidence in your players goes, what more could a coach ask for?

❖

The 1985–86 Texas Lady Longhorns was arguably one of the greatest women's college basketball teams ever assembled. Ole Miss had a huge task in trying to slow them down in front of more than 10 thousand fans in the hostile environment in Austin. ESPN and the entire women's basketball community were at that game in hopes of a great one. They got it.

Texas was very deep and they had a lot of great players on that team. But the Lady Rebels played their hearts out for forty minutes and executed every play Van had hoped. Ole Miss played with Texas right down to the end and Van couldn't have asked for anything more from his players.

The game went back and forth for forty minutes, but Texas went on to win their thirty-second straight game of the season, beating Ole Miss 66-63. The Longhorns went to the Final Four and won the national championship. They finished the season 34-0 and were the first women's college basketball team in NCAA history to go undefeated.

Even though Van lost that game and his second chance to go to the Final Four, it was an incredible jump-start for his career. The game was recently voted the greatest regional final game in the history of the women's NCAA tournament, and was featured in the 1998 Women's Final Four souvenir program. His team played well and people took notice that they were able to stay within three points of Texas. It was the first national television game for Van and the Ole Miss program, and the eyes of every college coach in America were peeled to this particular game.

When the game was over Van headed back to the locker room with his head hung and his ego bruised. They had come so close to pulling off the upset of the year and reaching the Final Four for the first time. With his head in his hands and the sweat and tears beginning to dry up after the loss, he couldn't believe what happened next. Because of the nature of the game, a lot of the Ole Miss administrators were in attendance that night in Austin. The university president, Gerald Turner, was one of them; he put his arm around Van and told him that despite the loss it was one of the greatest coaching jobs he had ever seen.

Turner was at a lot of Ole Miss games and he certainly didn't want to miss this one. Van thanked him and they began to walk, talking about the game. Later that evening, more school administrators congratulated Van and told him what a great job he had done despite the loss. Back at Ole Miss the following day, he got more of the same. Everywhere he went his friends and co-workers were bragging on him telling him what a great coaching job he had done against Texas. It was tough for Van to take; after all, their season was over, they lost the biggest game in the history of the program, and they failed to get to the Final Four for the second straight year, yet everyone continued to tell Van what a great coach he was. Just like any human being, after a while of everyone patting you on the back you really begin to believe it and Van started to think that he might not have been too bad a coach.

Coaches are a special breed and sometimes egos can get in the way, but anyone's ego would begin to swell after getting that much attention. Van loved it and a few days after the loss to Texas he headed to Jackson for the Mississippi High School Girl's Basketball Tournament. When he arrived at the Jackson Coliseum, the Mississippi State High School Athletic Association had a great seat waiting for him at the scorers table so he could scout new talent. But he wasn't about to sit down at courtside and watch the games when he knew that all his old high school coaching buddies were in the building.

Van got up and walked around the entire coliseum and let everyone he knew pat him on the back and tell him what a great coach he was. For three straight days he got nothing but "Hey Van, heck of a job of coaching against Texas," and "I saw you on ESPN—what a great coaching job." He was getting it from all directions and after a few days of that, Van went from thinking he was pretty good to knowing that he was one of the greatest coaches in America, one who could x-and-o with the best of them.

The drive from Jackson back to Oxford takes about three hours. By the time he got home, Van had convinced himself that he was clearly one of the greatest women's college basketball coaches of all time. He thought all he needed was some national publicity to let the rest of the sports world know how great he was. He got out of his car, went inside the house and called for his son Johnny.

"Johnny, I just wanna let you know that one of the greatest coaches of all time is about to take a nap," he told his son, who doubled as his manager that season. "Whatever you do, do not wake me. I don't care who or what it is, don't wake me. Can you handle that?"

"Don't worry dad, I can handle it. I promise I won't wake ya," Johnny replied.

But about ten minutes into Van's nap, Johnny started

pounding on the bedroom door and scared Van out of his deep sleep.

"Daddy, I know you told me not to wake you, but *Sports Illustrated* is on the phone and they want to talk to you," Johnny said. "Thank God, son. For the first time in your life, you done something right," Van told him.

Van's heart was racing, and he thought it was about time that *Sports Illustrated* woke up and realized what they'd been missing all these years. Van thought to himself that *S. I.* was going to scoop the story from everyone else and discover this diamond in the rough. Good for them, he thought, ESPN and all the networks were going to miss the next big story.

Van jumped across the bedroom and reached for the phone, almost pulling the unit completely out of the wall when he got there.

"Are you Van Chancellor?" asked the voice at the other end of the line.

"Yes ma'am I am," Van said with a smirk on his face.

"Mr. Chancellor, would you like to renew your subscription to *Sports Illustrated?*" the woman asked.

That was humbling, and from that point on Van promised himself to remain humble in victory and defeat. The 1985–86 team had quite a run in reaching the NCAA regional finals. For the second straight year Van was forty minutes away from reaching the Final Four, but for the second straight year he was forced to watch it on TV.

Although I got close and didn't reach the NCAA's ultimate goal two years in a row, I feel like I put my name on the coaching map and propelled myself to national recognition from my peers.

Chapter 6
Continuing the Tradition

VAN WAS TRUE TO HIS WORD when the 1985–86 season ended. He was still disturbed by the brush he received from the Ole Miss administration over the men's job, and he began to look at various coaching vacancies around the country. He had made a name for himself even though *Sports Illustrated* didn't put him on the cover. Everyone in women's college basketball knew who he was after he'd put together impressive back-to-back seasons.

If you put enough bobbers on the water, one is bound to go down; that was Van's game plan during the off-season. One of the bobbers did go down at Clemson University, and Van was close to leaving Ole Miss for the head coach's position with the Lady Tigers in the spring of 1986. Ole Miss was coming off another great season and had reached the NCAA regional finals for the second straight year. Van's stock was up, and when the head job opened at Clemson, the school contacted him regarding the position.

Clemson was a perfect situation for Van because it would have allowed him to keep coaching big-time college basketball and stay close to home in the Southern part of the United States. A final dig at Ole Miss was also in the cards as Clemson offered Van a $12,000 annual salary increase over what he was making in Oxford. But he wouldn't dare make a coaching move without Peggie, and in his negotiations with Clemson he got the school to give Peggie a $6000 annual bump in pay. She was a great recruiter, and every time Van started a fire, Peggie was there to put it out.

Van scheduled a meeting with Warner Alford to tell him about the Clemson position; on his way to Warner's office Van stopped by the break room in the Ole Miss athletic building. Peggie was inside preparing coffee when Van shouted from the doorway "I just turned you down a $6,000 per year pay raise."

"What are you talking about?" Peggie answered.

"Clemson offered me the job and a raise. They also said they'd give you $6,000 more per year, but I turned it down," he said calmly.

"The hell you did," Peggie screamed. Peggie is a born-again, strong Christian woman and her next swearword will be her first in many, many years, but in 1986 she meant what she said when responding to Van about Clemson. When Van told her about the Clemson offer, she dropped the coffeepot and the entire floor was covered in grounds and water and the room became an instant mess. "Good Lord, Peggie, I'm just teasin' ya," Van said, frantically grabbing paper towels. "I haven't turned anything down yet, I just wanted to see how you'd react. So . . . I take it you'd be interested in the move."

Her reaction gave Van confidence as he went into the meeting with Warner. Prior to the break room confrontation, Van didn't know how Peggie would react to the possibility of moving on to Clemson. But after talking to her he knew she was ready to go tomorrow, and it gave Van a lot of confidence when he told Warner than he and Peggie were ready to move.

Warner was stunned by the news. Immediately following the meeting, he sent Van to meet with President Turner to discuss the situation. Van told Turner that by 4:30 that afternoon he was either going to be the head women's coach at Ole Miss or the head women's coach at Clemson—it was up to him. If Ole Miss would match the Clemson offer for both him and Peggie, they would stay. Turner agreed to Van's $12,000 increase but balked at the $6,000 for Peggie.

"Van, give me one good reason I should give Peggie that big a pay increase," he said.

"I think, without question, that Peggie is the best recruiter on campus for this university," Van said, and stuck behind Peggie all the way. Van's loyalty was evident once again, because to him it's the most important attribute a person working in sports can have. He wasn't going to do anything without Peggie by his side, and he stood toe to toe with the university president and fought for Peggie.

"I thought I was the best recruiter on this campus," Turner replied with a grin.

"No disrespect, sir, but in my opinion I wouldn't trade Peggie Gillom for anyone," Van said confidently.

Turner finally agreed to the pay increase and the two stayed at Ole Miss. Van had a lot of leverage going into the meeting with Turner because of Clemson's great offer. Deep down, Van didn't want to leave, but all the signs were pointing toward a move to South Carolina. Betty was ready for a change, his dad was telling him to take the job, Peggie was obviously ready to leave, and Van still felt a little unappreciated for not getting a fair look at the men's job a year earlier.

If Ole Miss hadn't agreed to match the Clemson offer, Van would have been gone, because the pressure was on the university, not him. If the meeting with Turner had gone any other way, Van would have taken the attitude, "Fine, don't pay us, we're outta here and headed to Clemson." Fortunately it worked out at Ole Miss, and Van and Peggie concentrated less on their employment status and more on a loftier goal—getting the Lady Rebels to the Final Four.

With the Clemson situation behind him and the thought of leaving Ole Miss a distant memory, Van buckled down for the 1986–87 season. After a 24-8 record and a showdown with Texas in the regional finals the year before, Ole Miss picked up right where they left off. They won their first sixteen games of the season, finished at 24-3, and his team's solid play caught Van off guard again. In a three-year span from 1984–87, the Lady Rebels had a combined regular season record of 78-16, better than Van had ever hoped.

Ole Miss was a power in the SEC and in the nation again during the 1986–1987 season. It was their first year without Jennifer Gillom on the floor, and the expectations certainly weren't as high as a 24-3 finish. Without Gillom in the lineup the Lady Rebels were thin in the front court and relied heavily on their outside game. Alisa Scott was now the dominant player but she played primarily on the wing, and their offense had to adjust to her strengths. Van went from having a big, powerful team in the inside, to a small, guard-dominated team the following year. He had to make adjustments and they began to spread the floor and isolate Scott to give her more open shots.

Van would definitely miss Jennifer's talent on the floor, but more importantly he would miss her friendship and attitude *off* the floor. The Gilloms became a big part of the Chancellor family over the years, and Jennifer was a major factor. During her junior season, after a game against LSU, Van was upset with his team's play and made his frustrations known on the bus. He yelled at the entire team after the game and he pointed out Jennifer's lack of effort. When Van sat down, Peggie handed him a box score and told him he'd better look again. It was the one and only time Peggie stood up for her little sister in front of Van during her four years at Ole Miss. When Van looked over the box score, he realized he'd made a big mistake. Jennifer had a double double and one of her better games of the season.

"Jennifer, I owe you an apology—you had a heck of a game," Van told her later that evening.

"It's all right coach," she said. "I figured if you were telling me something, it was obvious that you were right and I was wrong." Van couldn't have asked for anything more out of a player.

Still, even without her on the 1986–1987 team, Ole Miss entered the NCAA tournament as a power, once again representing the SEC. They beat Penn State 80-75 in the opening round and faced Long Beach State in the Sweet 16 in Los Angeles. Although the Lady Rebels were good, they had no business being in the Sweet 16 against Long Beach State that year. They were completely outclassed, as Long Beach had a great team that season and finished with a record of 33-3. The Lady Rebels won twenty-five games and were a confident bunch of players, but that was the smallest team Van's ever been around. He knew Long Beach would stick it to them.

During that season, Donny Fuller, a graduate assistant who helped Van's coaching staff, did most of the advance scouting for the team throughout the season. He was getting geared up to break down Long Beach State just in case they should happen to get past Penn State. It was Donny's job to travel to various games of Lady Rebel opponents and then return to Ole Miss to formulate a scouting report for the coaching staff.

One day, Van and Jack Gadd were breaking down film on Penn State at Van's house, preparing for their first-round game. Van called Donny and told him that they needed some advance scouting done on Long Beach State in case they beat Penn State, and that he needed to send one of the coaches out to California to watch them play their opening-round game. Van told Donny that he'd also called Jack and told him the same information and that scouting Long Beach State was a huge responsibility and he didn't know whom to send. So, to be fair, Van told Donny that whoever got to his house first would be the one who got to go to California.

Before Van could say another word, Donny dropped the phone and raced to his car. Van hung up the phone and he and Jack started laughing because they knew the kid was doing everything he could to get to his house so he could make the trip to Long Beach. Donny flew through town and broke every Oxford traffic law in the book. He made the turn toward the house, saw Jack's truck in the driveway, and knew the two coaches were playing a joke on him because he clearly had the shorter distance to Van's house.

After giving Van and Jack a good laugh, Donny headed to Long Beach to scout a team that was far more talented than Ole Miss. But Donny did his job and was convinced he had a scouting report that could get Ole Miss past Long Beach State. Donny called back to Oxford just before the Penn State game. "If we get by Penn State tonight, don't worry, we're gonna beat Long Beach," he told Van.

Van admired Donny's enthusiasm but he knew before they even got to California that they didn't have a prayer. Van likes to surround himself with positive, enthusiastic people and Donny was one of them.

Long Beach State really put a number on Ole Miss in the Sweet 16 by the count of 94-55. They were down by nearly thirty at the end of the first half when Van looked down the bench toward Donny. Van had a look on his face that didn't need words. Before he could say anything, Donny looked up and said, "I'm man enough to admit I was wrong—I just can't believe it."

Van grinned and shrugged it off. He wasn't mad, but he knew, despite Donny's enthusiasm, that it would take a lot more than a scouting report to beat Long Beach State that year. After consecutive regional final appearances, Van had to settle for a Sweet 16 elimination in 1987. Although they didn't get another crack at the Final Four, Van was still happy with the state of the program. Many college basketball programs would have been happy with a Sweet 16 appearance, but at Ole Miss they'd set such a standard that a trip down that road was a shortcoming—and that was something Van could live with.

Up to that point, the thirty-nine-point drubbing by Long Beach State was the worst in Van's career at Ole Miss and is the second-worst defeat during his tenure with the Lady Rebels. Van knew on their way to California that it was going to be a short trip in regards to basketball, but he still wanted to make the best of the situation and let the team spend a couple of days in Hollywood. Although Long Beach State beat up on Ole Miss, the coaching staff was in a relatively good mood that evening and they rented a limo for an hour. When they got back to the hotel, Van had his son Johnny go to all the players' rooms to tell them that Billy D. Williams' limo was sitting out front and he wanted all the players to meet him. As the entire team gathered, and waited, and waited, and waited for the famous singer to appear, the sunroof slowly opened and Van popped out with his hands in the air and a grin on his face from ear to ear.

The moans and groans erupted from the crowd as Van stood in the sunroof, his coaching staff in stitches. It was a fitting way to end a great season, and an uncharacteristic way for Van to handle a thirty-nine-point whipping, which later became known by many on the Ole Miss campus as the 'Long Beach Massacre.' Van rejoices in victory and takes losses very hard, but on that night in Hollywood, the loss didn't bother Van as much as it could have.

Chuck Rounsaville, editor of the Ole Miss Alumni magazine, *Ole Miss Spirit,* wrote a story about Ole Miss' loss to Long Beach State and dubbed it the 'Long Beach Massacre.' Van and Chuck are good friends, but every time he referred to that game he insisted on calling it the 'Long Beach Massacre.' The story continued to surface in the magazine and it seemed every time Van opened it there was a reference to the massacre. Finally, after a year of reading about that game, Van laid it on the line for Chuck.

"Chuck, let me tell you something," Van told him one day as he read the *Spirit*. "If I read one more time about the 'Long Beach Massacre,' Mr. Rounsaville, I am never going to give you another piece of inside information about our team as long as I live. I am sick and tired of opening the *Ole Miss Spirit* and reading about the 'Long Beach Massacre.'" Chuck laughed, agreed and Van could finally put that dreaded game behind him.

❖

The following season Ole Miss had another great run and finished the season at 24-7, but again failed to get past the Sweet 16. That team also had to make adjustments, as Alisa Scott and Myra Williams, the captains from the 1986–87 team, were lost to graduation. Once again Van didn't think they had a team that could win twenty games, but tradition alone in the 1980s at Ole Miss won them games.

Van never thought they would win forty-nine games in the two years after Jennifer Gillom left, but once they started winning games in the late 1980s, they always found ways to win. Ole Miss players went into every game with a sense that they should win, and the Lady Rebels usually found a way to get it done. It was one of those times when a school had a strong program and the team continued to excel.

Ole Miss got off to a quick start again in the 1987–88 season, winning their first fifteen games and finishing the regular season at 22-5. Once again they entered the NCAA tournament as a solid team out of the SEC as they went 5-4 in conference play. Ole Miss played host to the University of Houston in the first round of the NCAA tournament.

Ironically, the head coach of the Cougars was Greg Williams, the current assistant coach for the WNBA's Detroit Shock, and former head coach of the Dallas Diamonds of the WBL, where Peggie played for one season in the early 1980s.

They had a huge, two-week gap between their first NCAA tournament game and their last regular season game. During those two weeks Van worked on every possible scenario that Houston might show them. They went over several plays, several offensive and defensive schemes, and Van felt like they were as ready as they were ever going to be for their first-round opponent. During that two-week stretch though, Peggie continually bugged Van about an out-of-bounds play that she was certain they would run. She knew Williams' coaching style from her days with him in the WBL, and was certain that at some point in the game they'd run this play. Van never reviewed it, never discussed it with his players and never brought it up in practice—until shoot-around the morning of the game.

Peggie continually nagged Van about this out-of-bounds play. He got so sick and tired of her asking him about it that he finally dropped his clipboard and walked off the court.

"Gang, listen up," Van said sarcastically. "Peggie is going to go over a play that the University of Houston is going to run late in the game, so we'd better be ready." Van's sarcasm was quite evident, but he was sick of it. He didn't think the play was that important, but in order to shut Peggie up he had to let her review the play with the team during the walk-through.

They practiced defending the play several times—more than usual—until Van felt he'd made his point. He thought they'd spent too much time on it already, but he really wanted to drive home that he wasn't happy wasting a lot of time at a shoot-around for a crucial game.

If Van ever listened to Peggie's advice, even just once a year, he always seemed to pick the right time. The Lady Rebels led 70-68 with twelve seconds remaining and Houston had the ball out-of-bounds near their basket when they called a final timeout.

"They're gonna run the play. They're gonna run the play," Peggie screamed in Van's ear as she jumped off the bench.

"I know they are, Peggie. I got it, just relax," he said.

"Ladies, they are going to run that backdoor play that we worked on earlier today," Van said in the sweaty, anxious huddle. "Do not defend any other play than the one we worked on this morning."

Houston didn't have a prayer of completing their backdoor play as four Ole Miss defenders were there to steal the entry pass. The play was defended perfectly and Ole Miss moved on to the Sweet 16. Williams had forgotten that Peggie played for him several years earlier; he certainly didn't expect anyone to know which play he was going to call in hopes of tying the game in the final stages. Peggie finally got through to Van; she had called it all the way and she still gives Van a hard time about that win.

Although the Lady Rebels got by Houston in the first round, they had to play Louisiana Tech in the Sweet 16 and were beaten 80-60, which ended another incredible year—a year no one, including Van, thought would muster twenty-four wins.

The 1988-89 season brought a lot of promise to Ole Miss as Kimsey O'Neil, a six-foot-two-inch sophomore post player, gave Ole Miss some height again, an element Van's teams had been lacking the two previous seasons. They were still relatively small, but O'Neil helped an inside game that had been nearly nonexistent in years past. Van was always put in a tough situation during recruiting times, and it was rare for him to get a player to come to Ole Miss from outside the Mississippi state line. Unlike most teams, Van wasn't able to recruit players to fit their style of play; instead he was forced to change his offense and defense to fit the recruits he was able to get.

When he was recruiting O'Neil out of Carthage, Mississippi High School, he asked his best friend in Oxford, J. W. Walker, what he thought of her.

"Well, if you're expecting O'Neil to take Gillom's place, you must be a heck of a lot better coach than I think you are," Walker said. "You know you're never going to be able to replace Gillom."

Van knew that, but he also knew that his inside game needed help. At the start of the 1988–89 season, Van preached to his team every day in practice about how they needed help in the post, and that it was the weakest part of their game. It angered O'Neil. She was one of Van's hardest-working players, accomplishing more with her ability than many who played for Van over the years at Ole Miss. Van brought out the best in her, and that's been his coaching style since day one. There were many days with the Comets when it looked like Van had a mutiny on his hands, but everything worked out the way he'd hoped. There were several occasions when Van had all eleven players mad at him, but they'd respond, and by the start of the next game the matter was dropped.

Along with O'Neil, Ole Miss had solid wing players in Jackie Martin, Cynthia Autry and Phyllis Stafford. They finished the regular season at 20-6 and 4-5 in the SEC and again had a solid team as they headed into the post-season. For the third time in his career at Ole Miss, Van had a shot at another Final Four when they played Auburn in the regional finals. And just like his two previous chances to reach college basketball's ultimate prize, Van had to face a hot team on their home court, as the regional finals were played in Auburn, Alabama.

In the Sweet 16 Ole Miss faced North Carolina State and won 68-63. In the meantime O'Neil tore ligaments in her knee, which forced her out of the game. She didn't play against Auburn in the regional final but Van still felt confident about their chances. Earlier in the season, the Lady Rebels lost by eight to Auburn, and Van thought on that particular night that he caught them in one of their better games. He thought they could make up the difference caused by O'Neil's absence, but five minutes into the game he knew they were in trouble. Without O'Neil in the game, Ole Miss wasn't nearly big enough, and the team was in serious need of her size against Auburn.

Unlike the first two losses he suffered in the regional finals against Western Kentucky in 1985 and Texas in 1986, Van was able to take this loss a little easier. He knew there was a reason they didn't get there in 1989 versus Auburn—an injury to their starting center had made them a much weaker team. But Van was so close, again, for the third time. He knew he'd built a power in the SEC—and in the country—during the 1980s, compiling a record of 216-60, which included three trips to the NCAA Final Eight and two trips to the Sweet 16. But he was unable to reach two goals that he'd always had at Ole Miss: a berth in the Final Four and an SEC Championship. In the 1990s, one of them was about to change.

❖

All college coaches feel like they have the toughest schedule in the world when first scanning their upcoming season. But Van might have a case for Ole Miss' luck, as they caught so many hot teams on the road during the 1980s. In their nine NCAA tournament appearances during the decade, their season ended six times on the opposing team's court and things didn't change in the new decade.

Ole Miss opened the 1990s with another trip to the Sweet 16, where they were defeated by Stanford, at Stanford, 78-65. Earlier in the tournament the Lady Rebels got past UNLV in the second round, though not many thought they had a chance—especially those in Las Vegas. Ole Miss finished the regular season at 19-8, but they hoped luck would be on their side in, well, Las Vegas, playing the Runnin' Rebels.

When the team landed in Vegas, Van grabbed a newspaper and read that a Las Vegas sportswriter had UNLV moving past Ole Miss in the second round and into the regional finals at Stanford. Ole Miss hadn't even played the game yet; heck they'd barely been on the ground five minutes and the women's basketball writer in Las Vegas already had UNLV beating Van and the Lady Rebels. But Van gave the writer one of the biggest snow jobs a week earlier when he interviewed Van over the phone about the game. No one in Vegas and the Big West Conference knew how good Ole Miss was, and the writer bought it. Ole Miss was clearly a lot better than everyone thought, and when they won 66-62, Van couldn't wait to find the sportswriter in the locker room after the game.

In a city where luck is a prerequisite, they got a bunch that night. Trailing UNLV by one with one minute remaining, Van told his team to run the five-play on the next possession. Van's notorious for having a lot of offensive sets and plays, and it can be confusing. A roadmap of the Los Angeles interstate system is probably easier to understand, but that's the way it's always been with him.

Van called the five-play, but by this time in the season there were several variations of the play: the five, the new five and the 'tide five' play, which was the new and improved five-play. Trailing by one when the play was called, two of the Ole Miss players ran the old five and two others ran the tide five. The team's point guard, Jackie Martin, saw the confusion and took it upon herself, drove to the basket and scored. Ole Miss hit free throws down the stretch to win by four, but if it weren't for Martin's quick thinking on that busted play, Ole Miss never would have been in a position to win.

On the way to the post-game press conference Van asked Jackie what they were going to tell the media about her shot and free throws that proved to be the game winner. "I say we tell 'em the truth," Martin said. "Well that sounds good to me, let's go with that," Van said, and the two sat in the press conference and told everyone that they won on a busted play. Coaching genius. Luck was, indeed, on Van's side that night, and if he was smart he would have immediately headed to the casino.

Martin was the true leader at Ole Miss during the early 1990's. She hit the shot that beat UNLV in the 1990 Sweet 16 and was *the* player for Ole Miss to start the 1990–91 season. But she suffered a season-ending injury early in the season, and they limped into the post-season with a 19-7 record. Stephen F. Austin eliminated them in the first round of the NCAA tournament and things looked dismal for the future of the program. The 1990–91 season might have been rough, but it was nothing compared to what Van thought was ahead for next year. He braced for a long, painful year for the 1991–92 season. He couldn't have been more wrong.

I worried about the 1991–92 season because I thought our program was on the decline. I worried for nothing—our team was actually peaking and I didn't even realize it.

Chapter 7
A Goal Attained

WHEN FANS THINK OF A POWERHOUSE women's college basketball team, one from the Southeastern Conference is sure to come to mind. A team from the SEC has qualified for the Final Four every year since the inception of the women's NCAA tournament. Of the eighteen national championship games, eleven of them have had an SEC team competing for the title.

So the goal of winning an SEC title was always a great priority for Van while he was at Ole Miss. An NCAA Final Four appearance and an SEC championship were certainly two lofty goals for a school set in tiny Oxford, Mississippi, but they were both goals that he thought were attainable. Van had several good teams at Ole Miss during his nineteen-year run, but never, never would he have guessed the 1991–92 team would go 11-0 in the SEC and win the conference championship—but they did.

It was one of Van's smallest teams during his tenure at Ole Miss. It was one of the tiniest teams Van's ever seen, let alone coached. They didn't have a center and they really didn't have anyone on the roster who would constitute a forward. Their tallest player, Clare Jackson, stood a mighty five-feet-ten-inches. Jackie Martin returned for her senior season at one wing and Charlotte Banks played at the other.

Kristen Goehring played a small forward position and Kim Gilcrest played at the point. Van tweaked the tiny lineup and installed a four-out and one-under offense, which meant they had four wing players and one player to post up inside. A small roster is an understatement.

When the season opened, Van thought they were in real trouble, and thought it was the year that the Lady Rebel basketball program would take a nosedive. On top of having a weak team, the Lady Rebels had one of their toughest schedules in school history, with Louisiana Tech added to an already loaded lineup that included playing in the incredibly tough SEC. He entered the season with his fingers crossed in hopes of twelve or thirteen wins, but they cruised through the entire schedule and amazed Van every time they took the floor. Ole Miss had a great run and finished the regular season at 26-1.

They opened the season with a win at Northeast Louisiana before traveling to the St. Mary's College Classic, in Moraga, California. Van was ecstatic that the St. Mary's Classic was on their schedule because he was banking on two easy wins over weak teams, such as Pacific and tiny St. Mary's College of California. He thought that they could at the very least get three easy wins to start the season before going to the Lady Techster tournament at Louisiana Tech, where they would surely take a beating. He hoped to get off to a 3-0 start with wins over Northeast Louisiana, Pacific and St. Mary's so they had a chance at salvaging a twelve- or thirteen-win season. He braced for the worst and hoped his easy early schedule would give them a respectable record.

The Lady Rebels did beat Pacific 74-58 to improve to 2-0 on the year, but St. Mary's College stunned them the following day. The shocking loss to St. Mary's was the low point of Van's career at Ole Miss. It was embarrassing to lose to such a small school and he knew that if they couldn't beat a team like St. Mary's they were in real, serious trouble.

St. Mary's has improved their program, and qualified for the NCAA tournament in 1999 with a 26-7 record, but in the early '90s they weren't nearly the team they are today. Ole Miss was so confident they would beat St. Mary's that Van and members of his coaching staff planned on watching the San Francisco 49ers host the New Orleans Saints the following day at Candlestick Park. The trip to California was supposed to be a mini-getaway for Van and his staff.

Peggie went back to Oxford with the team on Sunday following the St. Mary's defeat but Van stuck around to catch the 49ers game. He went with his other assistant Steve Curtis, the team's trainer Lynette Schwartz, and Sports Information Director Bonnie Bishop, because 49ers' tight end, Wesley Walls, was supposed to have left tickets for Schwartz at will-call. The loss a day earlier was eating at Van, but he went to the game anyway because the staff had planned on it all year. Besides, he knew that if he flew back with the team he would end up saying something he would later regret.

The way this trip was shaping up, it didn't come as a surprise that Walls hadn't left their tickets at will-call. Instead, the foursome bought scalped tickets at an inflated price and spent Sunday afternoon watching NFL football, with Van sitting all the while trying to figure out how he was going to get out of this mess called the Lady Rebel basketball program. As they passed their day at Candlestick, Van began to realize that he was never left alone—somebody from the Ole Miss party was with him wherever he went. If he had to use the restroom, Curtis was right by his side, and if he wanted a hot dog, he never went to the concession stand by himself. Finally, after the game, as they made their way back through the crowds toward the car, Van stopped and asked them why someone was with him wherever he went.

"We were scared to death you were going to jump off the back of the stadium," Curtis said. "The way you've been hanging your head all day, one of two things was bound to happen. You were either going to jump or you were going to fall off the back of the stadium because you had your head down all day and weren't paying attention to anything else you were doing." Although he was never going to jump off Candlestick Park, Van was still incredibly down; he needed to come up with a solution to the team's problems.

He had a hard time getting that loss out of his head as they flew back to Oxford. Van went back to Ole Miss on Monday and nearly ran the Lady Rebels to death during practice. The practice following the St. Mary's debacle, Van practiced them harder than any team he's ever coached before or since. He didn't talk to anyone on campus for nearly a week, and simply concentrated on making his basketball team better. At that point in the season he wasn't sure if they'd win another game, and the fearful possibility of a 2-25 season seemed very real.

Ole Miss was 2-1 and headed to the Louisiana Tech tournament in Ruston, Louisiana. The tournament is a four-team event. Louisiana Tech coach Leon Barmore tried to get Van to participate in it for many years, but Van always turned it down because of Ole Miss' already tough schedule each year. There was no need to play in such a difficult tournament early in the year with the SEC regular season right around the corner. But Van finally said yes to Barmore for the 1991–92 season and they made the trek west to Louisiana to face certain doom.

Van knew Barmore had been trying to get them to Ruston for the tournament for years; now that they were there, he had a feeling Barmore was going to drill them when Ole Miss was down. But Van said he wanted to take it like a man even though he knew it would drive him crazy.

Surprisingly, Van got an early eye-opener from the Lady Rebels when they played McNeese State in the first game of the Lady Techster tournament. Ole Miss had McNeese State down 29-3 in the first half and Van thought there might be hope to salvage something from the season. They dominated throughout the first half and led by thirty most of the way. But after Van made substitutions in the second half, McNeese State made a run at Ole Miss and they had to fight for their lives in the end to win by fifteen, 83-68. The game was much closer than the score indicated and it had Van worried that his team had blown such a huge lead.

It was a game they should have won by thirty or more; instead they let McNeese State back in the game. Van left the floor that night with his stomach in knots. He couldn't sleep, couldn't eat, and chewed more Rolaids than Newt Gingrich as a guest on the Howard Stern Show. He told Betty later that night that even though they'd had a great run at Ole Miss over the past several years, the Lady Rebel basketball program would never be the same again and that she'd better also brace for a long season. Despite the win to improve to 3-1, Van saw many flaws in his team's performance against McNeese State and he worried about the future—especially the immediate future—as they played mighty Louisiana Tech the next day.

Van takes losses as hard as any coach I've worked with, and it's weird that the win over McNeese State caused him more problems than many of the previous losses in his career. He hardly slept that night, couldn't watch TV in their tiny hotel room in Ruston, and spent most of the night pacing and thinking. Even though losses deprive Van of sleep, he usually gets some shuteye after he sits there long enough. But not that night in Ruston, after he saw his team stumble to the win over McNeese State. If nothing else it was baffling for Van, trying to figure this team out. They lost to tiny St. Mary's, responded with an incredible first half and opened a thirty-point edge over McNeese State, just to let it almost slip away.

He finally did doze off at about 2:00 AM, and awoke two

hours later when it finally hit him—they were playing too many players. It hit him like a bulldozer, and the longer he thought about it the more obvious it became. He realized that his players coming off the bench were the ones who lost the lead against McNeese State, and he later figured out that only about five or six players on their roster had enough talent to play quality minutes on the Division I level. He decided right then to play his starters against Louisiana Tech until they dropped. "I knew I had to play our starters until they just couldn't go another step, and if they died on the court, our plan was to call a timeout, revive them and kick 'em in the butt, because I just was not going to sub in that game," he said.

It was a tough decision for Van—one of the toughest he's ever had to make as a head coach because one of his substitute players was his daughter, Renee. She was a senior at the time and played sparingly at best during her senior season. Van felt she was good enough to play at that level, but just not good enough to play for that particular team. "It was an incredibly difficult situation but if you're going to coach, sometimes you have to make the tough decisions. They're not necessarily the decisions you want to make or that you like to make, but sometimes you have to face the hard choices," he said of benching his daughter. That was a tough choice, but his job was to win and he had to make the necessary adjustments.

Peggie agreed with his decision to play only the starters. So did Steve Curtis. Van felt a little better about his team the next morning now that he'd come to the realization that their subs couldn't keep pace. Although Van did feel better, he certainly didn't make any plane reservations for the post-season. He thought this was just a quick fix to get them through the season without embarrassing themselves. Van told Betty before the Louisiana Tech game that they were going to get beat badly, but that he might have found a solution to salvage at least fifteen wins on the season and keep them above the .500 mark.

Ole Miss entered the Louisiana Tech game as severe underdogs. Tech was coming off a 32-1 season in 1990 and had made a Final Four appearance after finishing the regular season ranked number one in the nation. They were definitely pre-season favorites to return to the Final Four. They entered the game against Ole Miss a little overconfident, but after watching them play the night before against McNeese State, who could blame them?

Van stuck to his promise to his coaches; they made very few substitution rotations the entire game against Tech. Before the game, Van addressed the team in the locker room and told them that he was upset with the way they had been playing and that he didn't expect anyone to play against Louisiana Tech except for the five who started the game.

Van talked to a roomful of long faces that night, but he meant it for the entire season. This wasn't going to be a one-night trial run of grasping at straws; this was now going to be law for the Lady Rebels for the remainder of the 1991–92 season. They played just seven players against Louisiana Tech, two of whom combined for three minutes and shocked the Lady Techsters 63-60—the first loss ever in the history of their own tournament.

Van was dumbfounded after beating Louisiana Tech in their place, at their tournament. After winning that game Van started to get his hopes up for a decent season but still had no idea that they were about to run the table in the SEC and not lose another game for the remainder of the regular season.

❖

Ole Miss won their next twenty-four games and finished a perfect 11-0 in the Southeastern Conference—the first team in the SEC to finish the conference season undefeated. And Ole Miss did it in dramatic style. Every Lady

Rebel conference game that year seemed to come down to the wire. Van got a lot more gray hair and noticeably shorter fingernails that season because every game was a dandy. The Lady Rebels marched through the SEC, but won all eleven games by an average margin of 8.1 points per game, which included their only blowout of the season against Georgia, 88-59.

Talking about that season still brings a curious look to Van's face—he doesn't know how they did it and every game was gut wrenching. Every time they took the floor, Van thought they'd get beat. Incredibly, there was a time earlier in the season when he didn't think they'd win ten games all year. He never dreamed they'd have a shot at going undefeated in the conference.

When Ole Miss was 3-0 in the conference, they played host to Tennessee, the perennial power in the SEC. As in most cases, college basketball fans trickled in midway through the women's game in preparation for the men's game to follow. On the night the Lady Rebels played Tennessee, the Ole Miss men followed with a game against Arkansas. Tad Smith Coliseum at Ole Miss slowly began to fill throughout the second half of the women's game, and those in attendance saw a great game that seesawed to the very end. Those glued to their seats to see the outcome included the Arkansas men's team, who stayed and watched until the final buzzer sounded.

Van apologized to Arkansas head coach Nolan Richardson for going into overtime and not giving his team enough time to warm up. But Richardson told Van he was all right with it because he enjoyed their game and didn't have the heart to tear his kids away from such a good one. Unfortunately, women's college basketball plays second fiddle to the men's program 90 percent of the time, so it was great for Van to have his team put on a show when they had a captive audience.

Ole Miss clinched the SEC at home on Feb. 29, 1992 when they squeaked by Vanderbilt 59-57. A loss would have given them a share of the SEC crown with Tennessee at 10-1. They came within a whisker of losing to Vanderbilt as they held the ball, trailing by two with just moments to play. Vanderbilt head coach Jim Foster, a good friend of Van's, asked for a timeout in the waning moments and Van told his players to watch for a screen to open a player on the top of the key for a three-pointer.

Foster called the play for former Detroit Shock guard Rhonda Blades, and Ole Miss read the screen perfectly. Kristen Goehring reached out and swatted the ball away at the buzzer and the Lady Rebels made history with a team Van would have guessed was going to be one of his worst if you'd asked him at the beginning of the season.

The Lady Rebels entered the SEC tournament and defeated Auburn in the first round but were quickly defeated the next night by Georgia, 71-60 which was their first loss in nearly three and a half months. Auburn was better than Ole Miss was and Van knew it. Even though they entered the game with a twenty-five-game winning streak, Van wasn't surprised by anything. He thought they'd get beat every game they played, so the Georgia loss didn't surprise him at all. He thought they could lose every time they took the floor, so when they kept winning he just went along for the ride. They lost just three games, but all three times Van expected it. It's ironic, but at one point in the season Van thought they might finish with three wins, not three losses.

A small team, they couldn't rebound to save their lives, but they could shoot. Van made adjustments at the start of the season and used the four-out and one-under offense until it became repetition. With four great shooters on the wings, someone was almost always certain to be open and fortunately for that four-month stretch called the 1991–92 season, they were in a zone. Van spread the offense, moved the ball around the floor and made the rest of the SEC guard them one-on-one. He tried it eleven times that year during the conference schedule and eleven times it worked.

The only thing that could stop them was if the Ole Miss shooters went cold. It had happened once at St. Mary's, in California, and it happened again against Georgia in the SEC tournament. But they recovered after the Georgia loss and began their march though the NCAA tournament, with a first-round victory over Southern Illinois, 72-56.

The following round they battled back from six down with under a minute to play to defeat Penn State, 75-72. That win sent them to the regional final for Van's fourth crack at an NCAA Final Four berth, but it also drained the life out of the Ole Miss players. Two days later, in his fourth chance to reach the Final Four, Southwest Missouri State stuck it to the Lady Rebels, drilling them 94-71.

For an entire season they got by on guts and grit and when they found themselves down to the bigger, more physical Southwest Missouri State team in the first half, they began to cave. The Ole Miss players were tired after the Penn State victory and they just couldn't keep up with Southwest Missouri State. Van realized he had missed his best shot at reaching the Final Four. When he saw they had Southwest Missouri State in their bracket, Van was confident they were headed to the Final Four because he was certain they could get past them. That loss bothered him because he didn't realize how much the Penn State game two days earlier would drain out of his team.

Southwest Missouri State's press became too much for Ole Miss, and for the first time all season they got into foul trouble. Van hated to reach for his bench, but the aggressiveness from his starters, which had won him so many games that season, finally caught up with him in the second half. Although they were down at halftime, Van still felt they had a shot at winning because they'd been notorious for erasing halftime deficits all year. But when the second half started and the deficit continued to grow, Van knew their great run of 1991–92 was just a matter of time from ending.

"I'll never forget that team," Van says of his 1991–92 team. "Those players were the smallest bunch I've ever been around. How we won twenty-nine games that year I'll never know."

❖

Little did Van know that the 1991–92 shot at a Final Four appearance would be his last. He coached for five more years at Ole Miss, only twice reaching the twenty-win plateau. Ole Miss' overall dominance in the regular season slowly diminished, and over those five years they had a combined regular season record of 92-41. Granted, 92-41 over a five-year stretch isn't too terribly bad, but Van had gotten accustomed to shattering the twenty-win mark and having a real shot at the national title. Over his last five seasons Ole Miss never made it out of the second round of the NCAA tournament, and the stresses of college coaching and recruiting started to weigh heavy on Van's abilities and desires.

After traveling the southern part of the United States for over fifteen years, looking for the best players he could find, the art of college recruiting began to take its toll. Van and Peggie would put all their efforts into signing quality players from the state of Mississippi, and for many years they were a lock for getting those players to commit to Ole Miss. But toward the end of his Ole Miss run, Van started to lose some of those great recruits to schools all over the country.

During their successful times at Ole Miss they signed a lot of solid high school players from Mississippi, but things started to die off for them toward the end. For one, the state of Mississippi didn't produce the number of good players that it had in the past, and the quality of high school basketball in the state decreased. It became a lot tougher in the 1990s to find Division I talent in Mississippi. The thing that really got Van down was being unable to sign the top two players in the state in back-to-back years, 1993 and 1994. Murriel Page signed with the University of Florida, and Passion Thompson signed with the University of Tennessee. Page is now a member of the Washington Mystics of the WNBA.

Page and Thompson were great post players and when Van was unable to sign them to his program, it really hurt. Not only did it hurt them on the court, it hurt Van personally because he felt like they always had such an advantage over other schools when trying to sign in-state talent. When he lost those two, his passion and confidence took a serious hit.

College women's basketball has changed so much since Van became involved in 1978, and recruiting is the best example of the change. More and more schools are becoming deeply involved in improving their women's basketball programs, and the task gets tougher and tougher each year. When Van started at Ole Miss in '78 there weren't more than fifteen schools in the entire country that emphasized women's college basketball. Today every school is making a real effort to improve its program because women's basketball is a great way to earn recognition for the school and its athletic department.

Van was tired of the recruiting fight and was ready for a new challenge. Early in 1996 he heard there was going to be a new women's professional basketball league in the United States, called the American Basketball League (ABL). Van began to wonder if coaching professional ball was something he wanted to pursue. He asked Betty her thoughts; she said if it was something he really wanted to do, then she was up for a change of scenery and he should go for it. Van began to research the ABL and, though their coaches were all in place for the 1996–97 season, he kept a close eye on the development of the league.

In the summer of 1996, Van was recruiting for Ole Miss at an AAU basketball tournament in Seattle when he first heard about the Women's National Basketball Association. The sound, "WNBA," really piqued his interest and he had a feeling this baby was going to fly.

"If David Stern and the owners of the NBA were behind this league, then it's got a shot," Van said. "I really thought it had a chance of being the first professional women's basketball league in the United States to make it, and I was really, really interested in becoming involved."

After he returned to Oxford from the AAU tournament, Van got on the phone with all his coaching friends and began to pick their brains about the WNBA and its potential success. He didn't have any idea who was running the league, or who to contact; he was just inquiring about the league and getting as much information about it as he could. He was casual and calm on the phone with his colleagues, but he was like a school kid again inside when he thought about the WNBA's potential. He was excited about the thought of coaching professional women's basketball, and he used to joke around with Peggie about heading up a new team. He would jump in her office at Ole Miss and ask, "Peggie, what's it gonna be like coaching in Dallas, or maybe Milwaukee?" He didn't have any idea where all the teams were going to be but he couldn't stop thinking about this new league and the possible career opportunities it presented.

Although the WNBA was in its early stages, Van knew he had enough information about it and he knew he was tired of college coaching and recruiting. He was ready for this league and thought it was time to make his run at a coaching job. There were eight teams in the WNBA's inaugural season and Van told six of them that he was interested in their head coach positions. He didn't think a small-town country boy from the fields of Mississippi could make it in New York or Los Angeles so he didn't bother showing an interest. But he and Betty put together a lengthy résumé and sent it to Sacramento, Utah, Phoenix, Cleveland, Charlotte, and Houston. He heard back from Charlotte and Houston.

If he was going to show a real interest in making this type of move, he had to be serious about it and make sure Betty was too. Van had it made at Ole Miss and if he was to move out of Mississippi, he was going to lose a large chunk of his state retirement, which was beginning to really take shape at his age. This was going to be a major move for a guy who'd never called anything outside the Mississippi state line his home. Still, the more he talked about the WNBA, the more excited he got about it. And the more excited he got about the WNBA, the more the recruiting started to drive him crazy.

Fortunately for Ole Miss and for Van, he signed all of his players early for the 1997–98 season and he stayed loyal to Ole Miss even though they knew he wanted to advance his career to the professional ranks. He signed all four of their scholarship athletes in November 1996 for the 1997–98 season because he didn't want other schools using his interest in the WNBA against him or the Ole Miss program. If you're battling with another coach over a recruit, you'll use any means possible to get that player to sign, and Van didn't want any potential player to think that his program was on shaky ground because he was looking to move on. Actually, Van wasn't sure if he was going to move on because the thought of making that big a move to the WNBA seemed almost overwhelming.

Van's family strongly encouraged him to make the change. Betty, his children, his brother and everyone close to him wanted him to make the move because they felt the pressure of recruiting was beginning to get to him. Van didn't think it at the time but they were right. He feels so much better now because the stress of recruiting is completely gone. He still feels pressure in the WNBA, but it's over wins and losses. At Ole Miss he had double the stress because they had to produce wins, of course, but their off-season was just as stressful, as they were banging on doors all across the country trying to get kids to come play for them. You won't find a bigger fan of the WNBA draft than Van—he picks 'em, they play.

Although Van sent resumes to six teams for the start of the WNBA in 1997, he still wasn't sure if he could make it living outside the comforts of Mississippi. But when Charlotte called wanting to interview him, he knew he was ready to take a serious look and another step in his career. Although the Van met with the Sting front office several times about the head coach position, it simply didn't work out and they couldn't find common ground. They parted company, but when Charlotte called initially, Van was incredibly excited and he knew that if they could have reached an agreement, he and Betty were North Carolina bound—no question about it.

The Charlotte position didn't materialize, but he soon got the biggest break of his professional career: Van's good friend Leon Barmore, of Louisiana Tech, decided he didn't want to be head coach of the Houston Comets. For whatever reason, Leon and the Comets couldn't get together. The reason didn't matter to Van because it gave him his big break.

"People sometimes ask me if it bothers me that I wasn't Houston's first choice, but I tell them I'm not so sure I was my wife's first choice either and we've been together for thirty-six wonderful years," Van said. "I really don't care what choice I was in Houston's hiring process, I'm just thankful to Comets owner Les Alexander and the rest of the Comets organization that I was their final choice."

Van was at a spring football practice at Ole Miss in early 1997 when he got word that Betty was frantically looking for him. It wasn't like Betty, and Van originally thought there was a family emergency. But she was trying to track him down because Carroll Dawson, the Rockets' Vice President of Basketball Operations, better known as CD, was on the line. CD and Van had talked previously about the head coach position with the Comets, and now he wanted Van to fly to Houston to meet with him and Rockets owner Les Alexander. They wanted to interview him one final time, as Van had met with Les two weeks earlier, in Boca Raton, Florida.

Van didn't want just any WNBA job. He wanted to win a championship and Les made it perfectly clear that a championship was his intention as well. Les didn't want a WNBA team just for the sake of having one; he wanted to add to his Rockets championships, and Van saw that commitment and knew he wanted to work for Les in Houston.

Houston made Van a great offer and he was almost certain he was going to take it, but he never makes a big move without first talking to his dad. He runs everything by his dad, and always has. While I was with Van in Houston, he would run things by me all the time, from the WNBA draft to what I thought about a potential trade, to which way he should drive home at night. But no matter what my answer was, his decision was never solidified until he reached for the phone and got in touch with his dad.

When Houston made their offer, Van dialed Louisville to tell his dad that he was thinking seriously about the job.

"Son, I just don't think I'd take that job if I were you," he told Van.

"Why not?" Van asked.

"Well, you just got it made at Ole Miss," his dad said. "You got an athletic director that doesn't bother you, you play golf every day, you do what you want when you want and all of your friends are in Oxford. You don't know a soul in Houston."

"You know, Dad, you may be right," Van said. "I think I will turn them down."

"By the way boy, how much money exactly are (we) turning down," Winston asked.

"Well Dad, they're offering me more money than I've ever made in my life," Van responded.

Without hesitating for a second, Van's dad replied, "Well hell son, with your personality, you can make a lot of friends in Houston, Texas!"

With his dad's blessing and the thought of coaching women's professional basketball in a league that he was sure was going to make it, Van and Betty loaded up the past nineteen years of Ole Miss memorabilia and headed to Houston. The decision wasn't made without a heavy heart, though. Ole Miss was good to Van for many years; he'd had a lot of success and had plenty of unforgettable memories. But he knew it was time for a change and a new experience. He had a good feeling about the WNBA, but he wasn't 100 percent sure if it was going to fly—no one was. But he was going to give it everything he had in Houston to make it a success.

"I felt like my career had been rejuvenated, and for the first time in many, many years I looked forward to a season with great anticipation thanks to the WNBA."

Growing up in Louisville, Mississippi, Van began his basketball career playing for his high school.

At the age of 23, Van was named the head coach at Horn Lake High School in Mississippi and led them to an overall record of 173-52 in six seasons.

Van (right) with his thoughts just moments before coaching his first game for the Ole Miss Lady Rebels in 1978.

Running out of shelf room... Above, Van with the first three WNBA Championship trophies. And below, Van holds the first three WNBA Coach of the Year Awards.

Three championships, three reasons... Van, with Cynthia Cooper, Tina Thompson and Sheryl Swoopes at Houston's 1998 Media Day, showing off their first championship trophies.

A tearful sendoff... Van say farewell to longtime assistan coach Peggie Gillom after a Comets victory midway thro the 1998 season.

Calm before the storm... With current assistant coach Alisa Scott, Van sits patiently on the bench anticipating the tip-off of a Comets game.

Post-game hug... Van doesn't go far without grandson Nicholas by his side.

Get the ball to who?... Van on the sidelines during seperate games with the Comets. We're betting Sheryl Swoopes was the recipient in the top photo and Cynthia Cooper's number was called in the bottom photo.

From Texas Tech to Houston... Van on the sidelines with one of the greatest players in the WNB
Sheryl Swoopes.

Words with the MVP... Three-time WNBA scoring champion and two-time league MVP Cynthia Cooper with Van during a game in 1998.

Fans Come First... Since coming to Houston in 1997, Van has always made time for Comets fans and fans of the WNBA. This photo was taken hours before tip-off at Compaq Center in Houston.

Spreading the Championship Cheer... Cynthia Cooper and Van sign autographs for the WNBA in Houston as the 1997 Championship Video is released.

Say it again, Coach... By the time this photo was taken in 1998, Brazilian Janeth Arcain was finally able to understand Van's deep southern drawl.

Heart and Soul of the Comets... Van a
Kim Perrot, who died of lung cancer
1999, became great friends off the co
and had a solid working relationship on
court, but it wasn't always that way.

The Leader and the Scorer... during the 1997 WNBA Semi-final game vs.
Charlotte, Van has a moment with Cynthia Cooper and Kim Perrot.

All-Star Break relief... Van had a great time at the 1999 WNBA All-Star Game, the first such event in the league's three-year history. It came at a time when Van and the rest of the Comets needed a break from an emotional season.

Unbelievable win... Van got emotional after the Comets' improbable come-from-behind victory in Game 2 of the 1998 WNBA Finals against Phoenix.

Working the officials... It's obvious what call Van is looking for as he works the officials during a Comets game.

Two biggest fans... Van with grandsons Nicholas (left) and Jacob before Game 2 of the 1999 WNBA Finals.

Championship Shower... The Comets finally got the celebration right as Van is drenched with champagne by Amaya Valdemoro in the locker room following Houston's victory in 1999. Houston was without champagne following the 1997 championship.

No. 3 for No. 10... Van and the rest of the Comets celebrate following the victory in Game 3 of the WNBA Finals against the New York Liberty. It was a game that capped an emotional run for Houston following the death of inspirational leader Kim Perrot just two weeks earlier.

The Best Feeling in Sport... Heading off the Compaq Center court following the 1999 championship, Van is engulfed in confetti as he waves to the 16,285 crazy fans in the stands.

All in the Family...
Three awards, two grandsons and a wife of 37 years.

What you play for... I'm leading Van to the press conference area following the 1998 WNBA Championship game. It turned out to be the last game we worked together.

Chapter 8
On to Houston

VAN INTERVIEWED AND ACCEPTED the Houston job on Friday, April 25, and the 1997 WNBA draft was Monday,
April 28. Needless to say he hit the ground running when
he accepted the job, and tried to find out as much as he
could about the players in the upcoming draft.

It was a huge surprise for Van to be in Houston. Although he thought about the WNBA all the time while he
was at Ole Miss, and was really excited about the possibilities, he still didn't know if he'd actually end up in the new
league. He was playing golf every day in Oxford and starting to enjoy the off-season and the summer vacation months
when CD called him from Houston. When he went to
interview, he wasn't sure if he was going to take the job even
if they offered it to him. He went to Houston pretty much
just to see what they had to say, and ended up accepting the
position. Betty told him before he left to take it if they
offered it, but he wasn't as optimistic as she was.

When he did finally accept, two days prior to the draft,
he was unprepared and knew he needed help. Kevin Cook,
an assistant coach with the women's team at the University
of Houston at the time, knew he could help, but Van told
him from day one that he had no chance of being hired as
his assistant coach with the Comets. Nonetheless, every-

where Van went Kevin insisted on tagging along and help-ing him in every way he could. Kevin wanted the assistant coaching job so badly that he stayed in Van's face for a month before Van hired him. But the first weekend Van was in Houston, Kevin was a huge help with the draft.

Kevin gave Van a breakdown on every player in the draft, and biographical information on almost every single one. Van liked the way Kevin was prepared, but told him on more than one occasion that as far as the assistant coach position, he was behind every women's college coach in America and every men's college coach Van knew. But that didn't sway Kevin. He just kept coming back and helping Van at every turn. Betty finally got angry at Van and told him that he should let Kevin go because she thought he was using Kevin and had no intention of hiring him.

I was with Van and Betty during the spring of 1997 when the Kevin Cook situation came up. Betty is a good woman, and she reiterated her displeasure with the way Van was using Kevin.   "Good Lord, Betty," Van said. "I've told the boy a hundred times he ain't gettin' the job. What else do you want me to do?"

On Saturday Van and Kevin spent the entire day to-gether, talking about the draft and the available players and different scenarios as to how the draft might play out. They talked nonstop about WNBA basketball and de-cided they needed a break. Van is a baseball fan and I swear he's bound and determined to visit every baseball park in the country. When I was on the road with him, he was always looking for baseball tickets in whichever city we were. We even stopped for a AAA game in Charlotte. On a trip in New York, Van jumped in a cab by himself and headed to the Bronx to catch a Yankees game. He bought a ticket, went to his seat, sat down for the first inning, and proceeded to do everything he could to get a better seat. When he got back to the hotel he couldn't wait to tell everyone about how he'd sat right behind home plate, in the Yankees' clubhouse. That's the thing about Van—he could have been digging ditches for a living and he *still* would have talked his way to a seat behind home plate at Yankee Stadium.

After he and Kevin talked about the draft all day Saturday, the two headed to the Astrodome to catch an Astros game that night, to help take their minds off the draft for a bit. It didn't work; they talked about the draft the entire way to the dome, the entire way inside the dome, through the seventh inning stretch and well into the post-game. Outside, they began searching for their car, realizing they didn't have a clue as to where they'd parked. Although they were at a baseball game that night, their minds were focused 100 percent on WNBA basketball. They walked around for a half-hour while Van pressed his alarm button, hoping they were close enough that the car would beep at them.

On Sunday, a day before the WNBA draft, Van had Kevin pick him up at the Renaissance Hotel near Compaq Center, which is in an area called Greenway Plaza, in Houston. CD wanted to meet Van and Kevin at the Rockets' and Comets' practice facility, Westside Tennis Club, on the extreme western edge of the city. Prior to the meeting with CD, Van took Betty's advice and told Kevin for the final time that he had absolutely no chance of being named assistant coach with the Comets, but he still appreciated his help. The seriousness in Van's tone and the sense that he had just wasted the better part of two weeks with Van rattled Kevin.

Despite the disappointing news, Kevin decided that he would still drive Van to the meeting at Westside, and told CD on the phone that he knew the way. Van and Kevin were supposed to be at Westside at 1:00; they finally showed up at 4:00. As the two drove aimlessly and hit every major freeway system in the entire state of Texas, Van knew Kevin wasn't the guy for him. He aggravated Van for three hours as he drove him all over the Houston area and Van let Kevin know his disgust.

"How could you ever think you could be my assistant when you can't even get me to my first meeting as the head coach of the Comets?" Van told him in the car. Van was so angry with Kevin that day. But later on in the three-hour car ride, Kevin fired right back at Van, asking him what driving a car had to do with coaching and scouting a basketball team. Kevin was right, and as time drew nearer to make a decision on an assistant coach, Van remembered what Kevin said and hired him one day before training camp opened. It was a great choice for Van and the Comets, as Kevin's worked his butt off to make Houston a better team. Van has since dubbed him the "Persistent Assistant" after Kevin's following Van around for nearly a month trying to convince him that he was the man for the job.

When Kevin finally did get Van to Westside that day, they were incredibly busy. Van sat in a conference room with two phones ringing in CD's office and a cellular phone ringing in each hand. He was talking with every college coach in America whom he trusted, asking for their opinions on certain players. They were flying that day as they got ready for the draft because they knew they had to put together a team the following day and needed some background information—quickly.

Van asked me for my opinion on many occasions. I told him honestly that, other than my sister back in South Dakota who played high school ball in the 1970s, I didn't know a thing about the women's game or its players. In my first working situation with our new head coach, that probably wasn't the smartest thing I could have said, but I've come around. You'd be hard pressed to find a bigger male fan of the WNBA than me or our former play-by-play announcer, Jim Kozimor, who's now play-by-play announcer in Sacramento with the Kings and Monarchs.

Amidst all the calls Van and Kevin were making and receiving, they got one from the WNBA informing them that Tina Thompson, from the University of Southern California, had just signed with the league. She was going to be available for the draft the following day, which changed things dramatically in the draft. Fortunately, Houston had the first pick in the draft because of a drawing held earlier in the year. When the league began in 1997, they had no way of determining a draft order so they took all eight teams and held a drawing. Houston was pulled first and it's pretty much where they've stayed ever since.

Van had only seen Tina play one time. She was a freshman at USC when he watched her on TV. He'd never seen her play in person and now they were faced with a dilemma: they couldn't make a decision about their number one draft pick. Not only was it incredibly important for the franchise, but for the history of the league. Houston would be making the first selection in the first-ever WNBA draft and their selection would go down in history as the first player ever drafted in a brand-new league. Everyone Van talked to said it was a no-brainer and that Tina was the obvious choice, but Van had his heart set on a veteran player before the Thompson announcement.

His first official day on the job with the Comets was draft day for the inaugural season. He knew a lot of the players listed on a draft board in Les Alexander's office at the Rockets' headquarters, at 2 Greenway Plaza in Houston, but there were a significant number of players he didn't know. That's one reason Van was happy Kevin was with him that day; Kevin seemed to know them all. Peggie Gillom, Cynthia Cooper, CD, and Adam Peakes, a former Comets front office employee who helped CD scout talent before Van was hired, were also in the room to help Van. The draft was also Cynthia's first act as a member of the Comets after she'd been assigned to the team by the WNBA weeks earlier.

Van went to bed that night fairly confident that Tina was going to be his top choice because so many of his closest colleagues had told him she was the real deal. They couldn't have been more right. Van called Les Alexander and told him about the top two choices for the draft pick and gave him the pros and cons of both players. Van told Les that he was leaning towards Tina, but with Sheryl Swoopes not on the roster the first season, he thought it might be a gamble to take such a young player. Les, too, thought Tina was the right choice and he told Van to go young.

"I knew she was the right choice after I talked with Les," he said. "He told me to go with the younger player and that even if it took us a little while longer to win a championship he'd stick with me. Goes to show ya' how wrong I was—we didn't have to wait at all for a championship and we know now that she was clearly the right choice."

That one draft choice has made more of a difference to her team than has any other draft pick by any other team in the league's short history. And she's also the perfect player to go down in history as the league's very first draft choice—a solid scorer and defender.

When Van woke up on Monday morning he still had that great feeling about Tina so he stuck with it. The night before, he'd talked with Jim Foster, of Vanderbilt, who'd done a lot of coaching for American traveling teams. Jim told Van it was his experience that older players don't bounce back quite as quickly as younger players after they've been hurt. What he said stayed with Van all Sunday night, and when he woke up the next day, he knew Tina was the choice.

When he got to the Rockets' front offices early Monday morning to prepare for the draft, the draft boards, player biographies and a cup of coffee were already waiting for him. No surprise—Kevin had beat him there by a good hour. At that time I didn't even know who Kevin Cook was. I thought he was just a guy helping Van out. For all I knew he was one of Van's assistants from Mississippi. I'll never forget that first day at the Rockets' front offices. Everybody in the place was curious about what we were doing in Les' office. A lot of my co-workers were more interested in this 'new' league and what I thought about it than in how we drafted. It's changed so much; Van can't walk through the front door without being mobbed by people in the Rockets' front office. He has an infectious personality and it didn't take long for it to stick with the Rockets' employees.

Van got to 2 Greenway early for the draft, and had a lot of time to discuss the team's four picks. The talk went around the room several times and the number one selection wasn't unanimous. It was split right down the middle between Thompson and the veteran player. Van said later that he knew all along that Thompson was the right choice. He finally shut down the discussion.

"Tina's our number one pick—end of discussion. Now let's move on to something else," he told the group. He was confident in the selection, but also nervous about the fact that he'd never seen her play. It was clearly one of his smartest moves since taking the job in Houston.

Before Van came to Houston, CD had the four main players in place. He had acquired Cynthia Cooper, Sheryl Swoopes, Wanda Guyton and Janeth Arcain through the league's allocation and Elite Draft. Without those four players the Comets would never have won a WNBA championship, let alone multiple titles. I've been with Van at several speaking engagements where he continually thanked CD for putting together such a strong core at the start. When Van added Tina to the mix through the draft, and Kim Perrot through the free-agency camp, he knew within a week after training camp started that he had a team that could be good enough to win a lot of games.

What a special time it was when the Comets franchise began to take shape that first year. Today the Comets are as much a part of the Rockets organization as the Rockets, but that wasn't always the case. The Comets are treated fairly and given as much attention as the Rockets are in the organization's front office. But it didn't get that way without a lot of hard work from both the coaches and the players. It's intriguing to see how far the Comets have come in just three years. The Rockets have been around for many years and have a rich history in Houston. But when you walk in the front offices, not only do you see huge photographs of Charles Barkley, Scottie Pippen and Hakeem Olajuwon, you also see a same-sized photograph of Cynthia Cooper driving to the basket.

But when we first started back in the spring of 1997, it was tough. The Rockets were in the midst of an NBA playoff run that eventually took them to the Western Conference Finals against Utah. It seemed everybody within the organization was keyed on the Rockets, and no one from the Comets could blame them. While the Rockets were making their run, Van and his newly formed team had to open camp and start getting ready for the inaugural season of the WNBA. The Rockets were obviously still in the middle of the playoffs and practicing every day at Westside, so Van had to find an alternate practice site. He finally ended up on the campus of Houston Baptist, and so began a franchise and its quest for a championship.

It's nice to see how far the Comets and the WNBA have come in Houston. Now, when the Rockets are eliminated from post-season play, the Comets are in the practice facility in a matter of days. I can recall running out of towels, practice jerseys and PowerAde in the early days at Houston Baptist. I used to sit on the stage in the school gymnasium during practice, working on everything from trying to create media attention for our team to trying to put together our game-night stats crew. There was a phone at the back of the stage, sitting on an old piano behind a curtain, and that's where I made most of my calls before the season ever started, trying to get everything together.

Van walked up to the stage one day after practice and saw me in the dark corner, leaning over the old piano, a phone in one ear and a mountain of paperwork at my feet.

"What could you possibly be doing up here," he asked.

"Did you see all the media at our practice today?" I asked him without looking up from my work.

"Boy, there wasn't a soul at our practice today—what are you talking about," he said.

"You noticed that? Good, because you're right. There wasn't a soul at our practice today, but that's gonna change," I said. "I'm doing my best to get them out here."

We finally did start getting some media to our practices at Houston Baptist after a week or so of training camp. It was tough, though, trying to get them to come out. I was pushing a women's professional basketball league and they were engrossed in the Rockets' playoff run. They had absolutely no interest in covering this "girl's league." There were many times when I called around, begging the local media to come take a look at this new team being assembled, and they didn't know if we were a softball team, bowling team or a member of the North American Tiddlywinks Association.

One of our first media visitors was Butch Alsandor, of KHOU-TV, Houston. When he walked in I immediately started making small talk with him about our team, our players, and the league. I slowly made my way over to Van in the middle of practice and whispered to him that we had a reporter here from Houston's CBS station.

"Peggie, take over," Van yelled from across the gym. He immediately had me point Butch out and Van made a bee-line to where he was sitting.

"Hi, I'm Van Chancellor, head coach of the Comets," Van said with his handshake extended for about twenty feet before he got to Butch. "I'm so glad you were able to make it out here today. If there's anything you need, anything at all, you just let me know. Heck, if you wannna pry that tie off and throw on some sneakers, you can come practice with us. I'm just happy you're here."

Butch stayed for most of the practice and they shot a piece for the ten o'clock news that evening. But it was tough on the media as well, because there wasn't a lot to talk about. We didn't have a complete roster, we didn't have uniforms, we barely even had a name, but Butch found an angle. He talked briefly with Cynthia Cooper, who at that time was just another player trying to make our team, and he talked with a few other players as well. But Butch's hook for the story was about the orange and white basketball the league was going to use. At that point, I was thrilled that we had a media member come to our practice. I didn't care what he talked about as long as it was positive.

Positive publicity in the spring of 1997 was a gold nugget for us. There were a number of media personalities in Houston and throughout the eight WNBA cities that were beating up on the league. Van and I talked the morning before practice one day about how bad it had gotten with some of the Houston sports radio shows.

"Guess what I heard this morning," Van said to me as the team was getting taped before practice. "The guy on the radio said that Comet was something you cleaned your toilet with, not something you waste your money on where the Rockets play basketball. Can you believe that?"

No, I couldn't. There were a lot of media people around the country who never even gave it a chance. Unfortunately, some still remain. But Van and I worked hard to change the attitude of *everyone* in Houston. I couldn't have asked for a better coach on this issue than Van. He was willing to do anything to get people interested and supporting the Comets—no questions asked, he just flat-out did it. And our players were the same way. They knew they had to sell the league to everyone including the media, and they made a lot of radio and TV appearances during training camp to help the cause.

We had Janeth Arcain on every Spanish-speaking radio station in Houston, and we had Tiffany Woosley, who grew up and played college basketball in Tennessee and is the definition of a country girl, on several country music radio stations. I tried to get Cynthia Cooper on any program that would take her because she was such a great interview and won the hearts of every person she talked to.

When the Rockets lost game six of the Western Conference Finals to Utah on John Stockton's last second three-pointer, Van and I kicked it into high gear. We knew we were now the only game in town and we did our best to piggyback on the Rockets' success as our inaugural season was now just weeks away. One of our staples during that spring was KNWS-TV, a cable station that featured a live program called "Sports Night Live." They were always looking for guests, and at that point in building the franchise, we were always looking to get on somewhere. Van agreed to go on the show. Everybody at the station loved him; they continued to call that first season and Van continued to appear. They were the only show that gave Van any real time during the spring of 1997 and he continues to appear on the show to this day to show his appreciation to host John Granato and the entire crew at KNWS.

But as the city turned its focus away from the Rockets, many didn't willingly accept the Comets the way KNWS did. Every Sunday night following NBC's local sports segment, Houston broadcaster Russ Small had his weekly segment entitled, "Small Talk." It was his 'video editorial' of sports in Houston, and he used his entire segment one night to bury the Comets. He berated the team, and finished by saying something to the effect of, "The Houston Comets are a waste of your time and your money and I don't see how any one could support it."

Van was mad after that, and ready to go to war. He called me and said, "Did you see that commentary on Channel 2 last night? I say we don't give the guy a credential for this year, not that he'd come anyway. I know—let's not give him a credential for next year's Rockets games. Better yet, let's invite him to a game, bring him out to half court before the game starts and let him play one-on-one with any of our players. That'll show him."

Russ Small has since come around to supporting the Comets. It's a good thing, because I think the fans of Houston would have run him out of town if he hadn't. The Comets have become so huge in Houston that I don't think anyone would dare say "Comets" and "waste of time" in the same sentence anymore. Van deserves much of the credit for this change in opinion. He worked as hard as anyone did to get this franchise off the ground. The people of Houston and the entire WNBA have seen his endearing qualities and they've rewarded him with their support.

His idea about challenging Russ Small to a one-on-one with a Comets player wasn't bad; I used it just a few days later. Ken Hoffman, a columnist for the *Houston Chronicle,* called one day to tell me he was going to write a story about the Comets and the players of the WNBA. I could sense this wasn't going to be a very positive story and I had a feeling it was headed toward, "Five average backyard bomber guys could still beat the best the WNBA has to offer." I suggested he come to our next practice, pick any player he wanted, play a game of one-on-one, and then write his story.

The next day he showed up with a pair of shorts, a pair of sneakers, and a pair of friends to watch and record him playing against a WNBA player. I walked up to him and said, "Glad you could make it. Pick any one of them, your choice."

"I want the little one," he said pointing to Kim Perrot. I pulled Kim aside and told her what was going on. "No pressure here, just my job," I said. She laughed, tied her shoes and promptly beat Ken 15-4. He wrote a great column the next day, which ran shortly before our first game of the season. Slowly we began to build momentum and though the negative press lingered, it wasn't nearly as bad and mean-spirited as it had been.

The real testament came just days before our home opener against Phoenix. From the time Van landed in Houston until the first jump ball, he worried about what our crowds were going to be like. He asked me every day where our season ticket base was at and what our opening crowd was projected to be. For most of training camp it was the same answer: not much change. We were just under 10 thousand tickets sold for the home opener with just under a week before the game.

The Rockets/Comets front office staff held a meeting at that time to rally for a final ticket push for the opener. They invited Van to help motivate all of the employees that were in attendance. Before he could hang up the phone, he was halfway to his car en route to 2 Greenway. Van was first on the agenda. His country-boy charm flowed through the room and he had everyone in stitches before he was done. By the time that group left the meeting, they were so fired up about selling Comets tickets that they couldn't get back to their desks quick enough.

It worked. In a little under a week, the ticket department and everyone associated with the front office—from broadcaster to receptionist—helped sell the place out; an audience16,285 strong saw history made on June 24 at Compaq Center. Selling tickets for a WNBA game that first year was a challenge. Van was incredibly proud to be associated with that effort in the final days before the first game. He referred to it many times throughout the season and he

knew the rest of the teams in the league now had a standard
by which to set their attendance goals.

*I came to Houston in May of 1997 and we had nothing. No
team, no jerseys, no interest and very little support. In two short
and unbelievable months, we built a franchise. It was an un-
matched collective effort from everyone within the organization. From Les Alexander, to John Thomas who ran the business team at the time, to the person who sold the very last ticket
to our home opener, we worked together to get that team going.
It's one of the proudest moments in my professional career.*

Chapter 9
Building a Franchise

THE COMETS' DAYS AT HOUSTON Baptist during training camp were memorable—times Van will never forget. It was somewhat comforting for him to be at Houston Baptist and away from the glitz and glamour of the NBA and the Rockets' push deep into the playoffs. Being away from all the playoff hype was good for Van and his team. It seemed to make sense to him that the Comets started where they did. The WNBA was a new league preparing for a sport that had failed miserably in the past in the United States. He felt like they had to earn their right to be at Westside Tennis Club and to be the main focus of the front office personnel within the Rockets organization.

Although it was a difficult task, training camp at Houston Baptist was also a lot of fun for Van. His nineteen years at Ole Miss had gotten incredibly repetitive. He did the same thing every year, every season, every day, every practice. His basketball camp was in the summer, he recruited like mad from April to August, and his team played its first game in October and prepared for the NCAA tournament every February. Now, instead of getting ready for another summer of recruiting at Ole Miss, he was in Houston, starting a brand-new franchise in a brand-new league that hadn't proved a thing. It was a risk but Van likes rolling the dice.

"We had fourteen players in training camp and I've never seen a collective group bust their butts more than those players did that spring," Van said.

Even though the WNBA hadn't proven itself, everybody associated with women's basketball had a feeling it would fly. Backed by the NBA, how could it not? All fourteen players knew it was going to succeed and all fourteen wanted to be a part of history when the Comets took the floor on opening night. Bodies were flying, elbows were being thrown and ability was being tested that spring in the Houston Baptist gymnasium as every player was fighting for a job. Each WNBA team was allowed to keep ten players on their "active" roster and two players on a "developmental" roster. The developmental players didn't travel with the team, but they were members of the inaugural season Houston Comets nonetheless. That meant two of the fourteen players in training camp weren't going to make the team, which meant a lot of fierce competition.

I'll never forget Patti Jo Hedges-Ward, from the University of Kentucky, that first year. Van brought her into Houston for a shot at the point guard position. She was a 1983 graduate and she brought her thirty-five-year-old body to training camp. Like Van, and many of the other players on the team, Patti Jo had seen how far women's basketball had come, and wanted desperately to be part of it. She battled throughout the entire training camp, but Van could tell from day one that she wouldn't be able to make the team.

During camp, the NBA had a film crew in every WNBA city to capture these historic moments. Following practice, the crew would take various players to a makeshift studio set up in the gymnasium weight room at HBU. During Patti Jo's interview, a simple question was asked: "Patti, you've been around this game a long time. What will it be like for you to take the floor in the first WNBA game?"

Patti Jo stopped, thought for a moment and began to get

teary-eyed. This was an emotional time, and though she never did get a chance to play in the WNBA, she was still a part of it and still helped make basketball history in the spring of 1997. After Patti Jo was done, Van and I walked out of the interview room and made our way to the exit. "You know, without even saying a word, she just summed up exactly how I'm feeling," Van said to me. He'd seen how far women's basketball had come and he was emotional during the entire training camp.

❖

Van used to live on the Mississippi Gulf Coast and he knows what hot and humid is. But Houston—Houston is a city as hot and humid as any place in the country. It took some getting used to that first spring, and the players had to adjust to the heat as well. It was the time of year when the Houston Baptist gymnasium was usually taking a break from activity. But the Comets were working hard and it got incredibly hot in that gymnasium with fourteen players flying around.

"I was so inspired by their effort," Van said of his training camp roster. "One of the toughest things I've ever done is make cuts that spring because I didn't want to kill a dream."

Van and his coaching staff had to trim the squad from fourteen to ten and that was difficult, but not nearly as difficult as making cuts in the free agency camp two weeks earlier at St. Thomas High School. There, the coaching staff had to choose four players to invite to the regular training camp out of the 200 hopefuls who showed up. The WNBA wanted each city to hold an "open tryout," or free agency camp, prior to the start of the first season. It was a PR move more than anything else because it created a lot of interest and every market in the WNBA had to take notice and it did get attention in the media.

Van invited some coaching friends to Houston to help him get through this huge task. Van didn't want to have an "open" free agency camp because he knew it would cause a nightmare, with so many players showing up wanting to play in the WNBA. But the league mandated it and he had no choice. He did hold out some hope that they might at least get lucky and find somebody out of this massive free agency camp who could make the roster. The Comets' roster was basically set, as the WNBA draft had already taken place. Within the first five minutes, he had the free agency camp trimmed from 200 to 100, and within the first hour he had that number down to about thirty. But it was a two-day tryout and, as the camp wound to a close, he realized he had to let some decent players go.

One player who didn't impress Van at all during the free agency camp was a little point guard from Houston named Kim Perrot. Van had absolutely no interest in her and didn't want her on his team. Every time she touched the ball during the camp, she made him nervous. She could shoot, make incredible moves, and get the ball to anyone on the court from her point guard position, but he just felt she could do more harm than good. She was reckless with the ball, and Van never felt comfortable when she touched it. Going into the first year of the WNBA with talented players from all over the world, he felt that he would need a solid point guard who could take care of the ball. Kim wasn't it—Van was more certain about that than anything else during those two days.

But every couple of hours during the free agency camp, Van and the invited coaches met in a classroom for a few minutes while giving the players a break. He went around the room and asked all the coaches to give him their top ten players. Every single one of them had Kim, not only in the top ten but also close to the top. He couldn't believe it and he stuck to his guns and didn't listen. He figured that sooner or later these coaches would see what he was seeing and Kim would eventually fall off their lists. She didn't—she just kept getting stronger and stronger in their opinions.

Eventually Van realized that he must be wrong. He had a lot of coaches with him whose opinions he valued and each one was telling him that Kim Perrot was the best point guard on the floor. He was the only one who didn't see it and he knew he couldn't be that smart, so Van took a chance on Kim and invited her to camp as one of the fourteen players to attempt to make the inaugural team.

She was in pre-season camp at Houston Baptist, but Van thought her only real chance of making the team was as a "developmental" player. In fact, odds were that she'd be one of the two players cut from the team because Van still had his doubts. But as camp drew on in the sweaty gymnasium at Houston Baptist, Kim started to impress Van. The minute she stepped on the floor, she added a dimension to the game, confusing opponents when she played defense and creating many open shots on offense.

The clincher for Van was the first pre-season game in franchise history, when Houston played the Charlotte Sting on the campus of Rice University. I didn't expect a thousand people to show up for this event but it was packed to the ceiling. We even had to turn people away, which was hard for Van to accept. I told him the day before the pre-season game that we were sold out and that it looked like we didn't have enough seats to accommodate everyone who wanted to come.

"What? First off, I can't believe we've sold this baby out, but secondly, I can't believe we're going to tell people they can't see us. We've been fighting for two months to get people to recognize us and now we're going to turn some fans away. Why don't we play it at The Summit?" It was a good thought, but the first season the league wanted each team to play their pre-season games away from their regular arenas.

Kim had a great game that night at Rice: she hit a couple of three-pointers, played great defense and, more importantly, sold Van on the fact that she was the player who was going to lead the offense. In just a few weeks she went from being an unknown, to making the fourteen-player camp roster, to being the starting point guard of the eventual champions of the inaugural WNBA season. She's an inspiration, and without her on Houston's roster the first two seasons, they would have struggled to win back-to-back championships.

But it wasn't always a love-love relationship between Van and Kim. They had a lot of problems the first season and had a hard time finding common ground. Kim had one style she wanted to play that drove Van nuts, and Van had a certain style he wanted her to play that drove her nuts.

"I coached Kim Perrot more poorly than any other player I'd ever coached in my life," Van said. "We didn't see common ground on a lot of issues on the basketball court, and her game suffered because I didn't let her utilize her best skills."

I remember several occasions when he would jump her immediately after something went wrong on the floor. Even if it wasn't her fault, Van was on her immediately and she was on the bench. After our third-ever game in 1997, Van was extremely mad at her and it was obvious the two had some issues to resolve. She played just six minutes while Tiffany Woosley played thirty-four minutes at the point. After the game, I jumped on the bus and Kim was sitting by herself with her face in her hands. She was obviously upset and wanted out of Houston.

But Van slowly started to see her best qualities and began to let her play her up-and-down, fast-paced game. "Coach, I promise ya' I can do more good than bad for this team," she repeatedly told Van. Eventually they found that common ground and it was a perfect match after they ironed out their problems midway through the first year.

❖

Now that Van had his team set and the season was closing in, it was time for us to officially introduce the team to the public at our media day. When I took the job in March 1997, I knew that selling a new women's professional basketball team to the public was going to be a challenge. I wanted to blindside Houston with this new team, and the last thing I thought we should do was hold a regular, boring media day at the Compaq Center or Westside. After much discussion with other people in our front office, we decided on NASA's Space Center Houston.

I told Van our plans and he was all for it, yet a little concerned as to its location. It was a legitimate concern because Space Center Houston is a hike from downtown Houston. Our biggest risk in having it so far away was getting the media to drive that distance to cover a team that hadn't played a game and hadn't proven a thing. Needless to say, I was nervous the night before media day. I felt like our franchise depended upon it and in order to get off to a good start in Houston, we had to make a huge splash in the media at least once before our first game.

I got together with the coaching staff the night before media day and explained everything that was expected of them. The team was scheduled to practice in the morning, jump in two vans we had waiting for them and then head out to Space Center Houston. Van was to drive one vehicle, Peggie the other. I knew Van didn't enjoy driving in the Houston traffic, and the thought of him driving half the team to media day worried me. I wasn't sure I'd ever see them again. Van told the *Houston Chronicle* shortly after taking the job, "A traffic jam in Oxford, Mississippi is getting in the wrong turning lane at Kroger. A traffic jam in Houston is getting in your car." I knew the traffic scared him, which, in turn scared me.

I got to Space Center Houston extremely early that day with my assistant Renee Costantino. I was nervous and wanted to make sure everything was in place for this big day. We clearly got there too early and I'm sure Renee cussed me out more than once over the early arrival, but we were ready—all we needed was a team.

As time drew closer for the team's arrival, I walked out to the Space Center parking lot and got on my cell phone to Van. First off, I wanted to see if he was on time, and secondly, I wanted to make sure that he was still within the state line.

"Hello," Van said as I fought to hear him through the static of the cell phone.

"Is this Van?" I asked.

"You got him," came an excited voice on the other end.

"Hey Van, this is Tom. You just about here? We're getting close and everything is ready to go," I said praying for a positive answer.

"Well, to be honest with ya' son, I'm not entirely sure where I'm at," he said.

I couldn't believe it. I thought to myself, we'd gone to such great lengths to make sure everything was going to go perfect and this guy couldn't even get the team to our first press event. I knew we had a situation on our hands, because I'd only been in Houston a few months, so I wasn't going to be much help giving directions. I thought I'd give it a shot because I'd made the trip back and fourth from Space Center Houston many times in preparation for media day.

"Do you have any idea where you're at?" I asked.

"I think I saw an 83 a second ago," Van said.

An 83? I'd never heard of any 83 the entire time I was in Houston and I was scared to death he'd driven completely out of the Houston city limits and was driving half our team around on some rural highway. I paced back and forth in the parking lot with my head down and the cell phone glued to my ear.

"Hey Tom," Van said behind a hidden laugh. "Look up."

I looked up and saw him sitting in the van about thirty feet away and the entire team was busting up. I didn't know if I should laugh or go up and strangle him. Our working relationship was in its infancy at that time, but after that stunt I knew where I stood.

"I just wanted to ease you up a bit," Van said as he made his way out of the van and into Space Center Houston. "You seemed a little tense over the last day-and-a-half worrying about this thing. Relax, we got it."

Media day was memorable and it couldn't have been at a better place than Space Center Houston. It's really a neat place and I think it was the first time since the entire team showed up for training camp that they enjoyed themselves. We introduced the team from the Space Shuttle in the middle of the museum. As each player was introduced, she made her way down from the Shuttle, surrounded by smoke, lights and blaring music. We had all the Houston media in attendance and thankfully we had a lot of kids there too. It was the end of the school year and we happened to get lucky that some schools were on field trips at Space Center Houston on the same day.

After Van was introduced and the entire team stood on the stage for a moment for a photo opportunity with the Space Shuttle in the background, Van grabbed the microphone.

"I can't tell ya' how excited I am to be here in Houston, coaching this team," he said. "I'm so happy that all of the media showed up here today. Let me extend this invitation to everyone working in the media. Our practices will always be open to you and you can talk to me anytime. If you're under the gun and need to meet a deadline, you just come get me and I'll talk to you. I don't care if it's the middle of practice, you come get me because we want to accommodate you and make you happy."

I stood there with my mouth open because I couldn't believe

he was making these promises. What he was guaranteeing the media was unheard of, but he meant it. Actually I couldn't ask for a better situation—there were no rules and our team and coaching staff were fair game for the media. It was refreshing to work with a coach whose ego didn't get in the way. He was there to win games and sell his team and I had a blast doing it with him.

Media day at Space Center Houston was a great success, which almost surprised me because the team's "Superstar" couldn't be there. At that time in the history of the WNBA, no one on the planet knew how good Cynthia Cooper was and no one could have ever guessed how big she would eventually become. At media day 1997, the entire franchise was Sheryl Swoopes. I announced our media day dates and times to the media at a Rockets game in late March. When I placed the information in our media lounge at Compaq Center, I could barely make my way out of the room without someone asking about Sheryl.

I was encouraged by their interest but I was also worried about the turnout for media day because I knew Sheryl wouldn't be there; she was seven months pregnant with her first child. I wanted her there and Van wanted her there, if only to meet her. It seemed strange that we introduced the Comets to the public and the player who was marketed by the WNBA as hard as anyone couldn't be there. When she finally did arrive to watch a Comets game shortly after giving birth to Jordan, Van had his first chance to meet her with the season already underway. Their friendship has grown from that point on as they've always had something in common: Jordan is two months older than Van's grandson, Nicholas, and he and Sheryl have compared notes the entire way on the little guys' progress.

❖

Once we got the hype and the preseason out of the way, it was time to go after the first WNBA championship. Houston started sluggishly and at one point was 6-4, which included three losses to the New York Liberty. Despite the mediocre record, the Comets were good; Van knew he had loads of talent on the floor every night but he couldn't get the offense jump-started. Midway through the year, we were in Sacramento when Van called Cynthia Cooper to his room the night before a game.

"I need you to become more involved in the offense," Van told her. For as much as Cynthia has accomplished over the first three years of the WNBA, it's strange now to look back and imagine Van asking her to do more. But Cynthia was hesitant on the offensive end of the floor early in 1997 and Van needed her to score. He told her that night that she was one of the best passers he'd ever been around and he couldn't remember a player who made people around her play so much better. He knew that for the Comets to have any chance of making a playoff run, Cynthia had to become *the* player on offense.

After their powwow in Sacramento, Cooper scored thirty points against the Monarchs the following night, which at that time was a league high. Van's words obviously sunk in, because over the next seven games Cynthia scored 32, 44, 21, 34, 15, 30 and 34 points. The 44 points came exactly one week later in Sacramento and is still the single-game high in the league's three-year history. Before Van and Cynthia got together, the Comets were 7-5 on the season and were averaging 69.6 points per game. After their talk, the Comets finished out the season with an 11-5 mark and the team averaged 74.6 points per game. Cynthia took Van's words to heart that night in Sacramento and hasn't looked back; she's been the scoring champion in all three WNBA seasons.

Just before the start of the 1997 playoffs, Cynthia was named the Most Valuable Player of the WNBA. Van was also named the WNBA Coach of the Year after leading the Comets to the best record in the eight-team league. The

WNBA decided to have a press conference announcing both the MVP and Coach of the Year award winners at the same time. It was one day before our semifinal game against Charlotte, and most of the WNBA VIPs were in town, including President Val Ackerman.

Van accepted his award first and was very gracious at the podium, thanking all the appropriate people.

"But now let's get down to the serious stuff," he said with a grin on his face. "Don't tell me this isn't a player's league. I get named Coach of Year, and I'm very grateful, but all I got was this here trophy in my hand. Don't get me wrong, I like it, I think it's beautiful, but look at what they're about to give the MVP," Van said as he pointed to a brand-new Buick Regal that was sitting next to the stage. "The least you could do, Cooper, is give me a ride in it from time to time. You know you're a heck of a player because of the coach you have."

The entire room was laughing, including Cynthia when she got to the stage. "Don't worry coach, you'll be my first passenger," she said. When she was finished accepting the MVP honor and was presented with the keys to her new car, Van jumped in the passenger seat and he and Cynthia drove away from the press conference. He wasn't kidding— he wanted the first ride!

The Comets were actually 18-8 at one point in the regular season but lost their final two games of the regular season, both at home to Cleveland and Sacramento. The final game of the season, a 68-58 loss to the Monarchs, really bothered Van even though they'd already secured the number one seed throughout the playoffs. In the press conference area after the game, he and his coaching staff paced and chewed their fingernails until there was nothing left. I couldn't believe it bothered them that much; our starters played limited minutes in a game that meant absolutely nothing to either team.

After the players had showered and were getting ready to leave, Van called Cynthia and Tina Thompson to the court. Compaq Center was completely empty at that point, but the two players stuck around and talked with Van. He pulled three chairs from the bench and placed them on the court, just off the free throw line. The three sat in the dimly lit arena for close to an hour, and every time I stuck my head out to see if they were still there, I could see the playoff wheels turning for each of them.

"I told them that I think these two losses to finish out the season may have just won us a championship," Van said. "We may not be as good as we think we are, just ask Cleveland and Sacramento." Maybe they weren't. Van talks briefly about that conversation with Cynthia and Tina, but whatever he said worked. They were as relaxed in the playoffs as I'd ever seen them, and they rolled through the post-season to win the first championship.

Even though they'd come a long way in four short months, the Comets still had growing to do. After they won the inaugural championship, the team gathered in the locker room and were screaming and yelling, but something was obviously missing. Possibly for the first time in the modern era, a professional sports team won a championship and was celebrating in the locker room without champagne. It almost seemed uncomfortable and Van had one of the ball girls turn down the blaring stereo.

"All right gang, great game," Van said. He started giving his post-game speech just like it was any other game. "I guess tomorrow we'll have a team meeting at Westside and we can discuss…"

"Wait a second coach," Cynthia interrupted. "We just won the dang thing. Let's stop talking about basketball and start celebrating."

"Okay, I guess we'll have a voluntary meeting at Westside tomorrow at 2:00—carry on," Van said. The words had barely gotten out of his mouth when the stereo was blasting again and the players kept the celebration going as best they could.

After the Rockets won the championship in 1994 and 1995 there was a huge parade in downtown Houston, where hundreds of thousands of fans packed the streets, hung out of parking garages and threw confetti from the tops of sky-scrapers. But after the Comets won the inaugural championship, the front office team decided to have a rally on the steps of City Hall rather than a parade. It was the right decision. As far as the Comets had come and as big as they had gotten, they hadn't gotten quite big enough to merit a full-scale parade. There were too many risks involved and a light turnout would have set the franchise back.

The rally at City Hall was a great success and the place was jammed. Van grabbed the microphone and quieted the crowd.

"About four months ago we introduced our team to Houston at a media event at Space Center Houston. There weren't very many fans there that day but we've done our best to make sure everybody knows who we are now," he yelled. The crowd went wild. "We've had a great season this year and there were many times when it didn't look good for the Comets, but you got us through the tough times. This championship is for you!"

That was the moment when I thought Van really began to win the fans of Houston and the WNBA. He thanked them and he meant it. From the moment he landed in Houston and took the job, he was doing everything he could to make friends with potential Comets fans. Even if people had no interest in women's basketball or had no desire to meet Van, they remembered him everywhere he went.

Obviously everything was new the first year. From the free agency camp, to the training camp, to the first game, to the first championship, to the locker room celebration, to the rally on the steps of City Hall. A lot of our players left immediately following the championship, heading home or directly overseas to join their European league teams, whose seasons started almost immediately after the WNBA season was over. It was a strange yet fitting end to the first WNBA season. We went into it blindfolded and when it was over, Van and only a portion of his team stood in downtown Houston with a championship trophy in their hands.

We learned a lot in the first year, but I had a blast the entire time. It was a ride I was so thankful to be on and for the first time in my life I didn't regret making a move to another coaching position. Houston was where I belonged.

Chapter 10
Defending the Championship

VAN KNEW WE'D MADE AN IMPACT on the WNBA and especially in Houston following the inaugural season championship, but he wasn't expecting the overwhelming response
we got during the off-season. I'll never forget how loud
Compaq Center got during our championship game that
first year, and Van and I made it a goal to continue that
enthusiasm now that the first season was over and the nov-
elty of the league had a chance to wear off.

The Comets season ticket base was great following the first
year, but we wanted to capitalize on the momentum of the first
championship, so Van and I hit the streets of Houston and the
surrounding areas. I scheduled as many speaking engagements
for him as I could and Van spoke at every imaginable civic
group and organization in the greater Houston area for the
next six months, doing his best to create more awareness of the
Comets and the WNBA.

Every week the scenario was the same: I'd schedule as
many luncheons as I could, Van would pick up a member of
our ticket department and me at 2 Greenway, and within a
matter of minutes we were at our destination, videos and
ticket brochures in hand. Every day was an adventure as
Van spoke to a group of business leaders, or at a school rally,
or to a handful of old ladies at a church, or on more than

one occasion testing his vocal chords, singing "America the Beautiful" at a Kiwanis Club.

Van should have been relaxing during that time as it was his off-season, but he didn't. He wanted to make the Comets bigger and better and he never complained—well, maybe once he complained. Van really liked the luncheons because he liked to get appearances out of the way early in the day. He likes spending time with his family in the evening and he asked me more than once to not schedule any night appearances.

There were times, however, when I was in a bind and just had to schedule an evening appearance. When I started doing the scheduling for Van, I grabbed a list of civic organizations in the Houston area and started dialing. I scheduled as many as I could as quickly as I could and inevitably I double-booked a noon luncheon. I made it up to the group we had to cancel by telling them we would join them at their next meeting, which happened to take place at night.

Van picked me up as the sun was setting and we made our way there. I was notorious that year for getting us close to where we needed to go, just not exactly where we needed to be. We got in the car that night and headed to the appearance and I had a general idea of where we were going. Again, I got us close, but I wasn't exactly sure in which building the meeting was taking place.

"Savage, I gotta be honest with ya', I'm getting a little sick and tired of getting lost," Van said as we walked around a church in the dead of night. "I mean aren't you tired of not knowing exactly where we're supposed to be?"

He was right, but c'mon! I was new to Houston too, and thought I was a genius for even getting us in the right quadrant of the city. We finally found where we were supposed to be and I found my contact in the hallway. Our appearances that year were hit and miss. As I made my way down the list while scheduling, I had no way of knowing what we were getting ourselves into. As Van and I stood in the hallway, it was evident this wasn't going to be one of our most productive meetings. As most of the audience was wheeled into the fellowship hall of the church, Van just looked at me with the corners of his mouth and his eyebrows raised.

Before he was introduced to speak, they took a snack break, and Van and I participated in the weekly ritual. As we ate stale cookies and drank orange soda, I knew he was fuming and wanted to finish this thing as quickly as he could. It's unfortunate, because when he finally did get a chance to speak to the fifteen who had gathered, their hearing aids turned up, it was one of his best performances of the year. Too bad the audience didn't have a clue as to what he was talking about.

Things weren't always that way though. Most of the time he spoke to packed houses and he never left one of them until he had signed every autograph asked of him. There were many days when we had other appointments to attend and we ran late because he wouldn't leave until everyone who wanted his signature got one. But not all his appearances were in front of live audiences. We also tried to get him on as many radio and TV shows as possible and every time we came up with one he did it.

Even if it was early in the morning, Van was willing to help the Comets. I scheduled a radio interview on KHMX-FM 96.5 in Houston on their morning drive-time show, where Van was scheduled to be on the "Larry and Shelby Show." We got to the station just before eight o'clock. Van was great on the show; he had the hosts and callers laughing the entire time. When the segment was winding down, they asked him to answer three multiple-choice questions. If he got all three right he'd win two tickets to a production of "A Christmas Carol." He couldn't have cared less about the tickets, and the blood rushed from his face and he turned a pale shade of white when they asked him to answer three questions.

As they were preparing the questions for him, I walked behind Larry and Shelby. I was facing Van and the hosts couldn't see me. I thought I would try to help him out, just hoping I might have a clue to the answers. The first question: "Van, who wrote the book *The Old Man and the Sea*? Was it A) John Grisham, B) Ernest Hemingway, or C) John Steinbeck?" Van was looking down during the question, but slowly looked up as the choices were presented to him. I stood behind Larry and Shelby with two fingers held close to my body.

"Boys, I'm gonna go with B," Van said with confidence.

"That's absolutely correct; Ernest Hemingway," Larry said.

"All right, Van, question number two. "Let's go to a little music, since we're at a radio station. Okay Van, who sang the song "Paperback Writer?" Was it A) The Beatles, B) Elvis Presley or C) Billy Idol?"

At this point I wasn't sure if Van knew the answer and I certainly didn't want to insult him, but I still stuck one finger in the air. "Good Lord, gang. I like the Oldies and Goldies, no disrespect to your radio station. I'm just playing with ya. I don't want to make anybody mad. Y'all got a fine radio station here. But to get to your answer, I'm gonna have to go with number one."

"Hey, you're two-for-two," Larry said. "The Beatles recorded "Paperback Writer." All right, this is too easy. Here's your third question: You ready for this one?"

"Bring it on Larry—I'm gonna get me a couple tickets to that play," Van said as he squirmed excitedly in his chair, a big grin on his face. He loved the fact that we were pulling a fast one on the station. He was ready for any question— except the one he got.

"All right, here you go. In chemistry, what is the symbol for Sodium on the Periodic Table of Elements? Is it A) Mg, B) Rb or C) Na?"

Excuse me? From the moment Larry said "chemistry" I

knew I was in trouble and had absolutely no chance of helping Van. He was on his own. I couldn't even take a guess, so I gave him a pair of shrugged shoulders, a blank look on my face.

With as much confidence as ever, Van replied, "This is hardly even fair fellas, but I'm gonna say C, then I'm gonna take my tickets and go to the show." Larry and Shelby were laughing so hard they could barely get the answer out. I don't know if they were laughing because of the difficulty of the question, the way Van answered it or because he got it right. Whatever they were laughing at, I didn't care. I was just happy they were laughing and I'm sure everybody listening that day was laughing as well.

Doing all those appearances was a grind and it wasn't easy for Van to get up three or four times a week to speak in front of large crowds. Luckily we had a break in January as the WNBA was incorporated into the NBA's All-Star break festivities. The NBA eliminated the Slam-Dunk Contest from its All-Star exhibitions and added the Two-Ball Challenge. Each WNBA city had a team entered and the Houston team of Clyde Drexler and Cynthia Cooper was going to give a solid performance.

Van was chosen as the coach of Houston's Two-Ball team and the three took it seriously. They practiced at Westside a lot before they headed to New York for the All-Star game. Van's job as coach was to make sure that Clyde or Cynthia scored from each of the designated spots on the floor. All right, so it wasn't the toughest job in the world, but Van was more than willing to participate. Obviously, it was the first time the WNBA and NBA had performed together on the floor, and again history was being made.

The NBA wanted to take photos of as much as they could. Before the game each team was professionally photographed. Van was like a little kid during the entire photo session. He, Cynthia Cooper and Clyde Drexler were on display for everyone to see. Earvin "Magic" Johnson was the coach of the Los Angeles entry, and Van knew he was in big company.

"Can you believe this, boy?" he said to me before the Two-ball event. "I'm coaching against Magic Johnson. Magic Johnson! My friends back in Mississippi will never believe this. I couldn't even make this stuff up."

Clyde and Cynthia were dead-on in the final round and ran away with the victory. It seemed every event the WNBA could come up with, Van and the Comets were coming away victors. It hasn't changed. In the press conference following the Two-Ball victory, Van sat down, looked over the massive assembled media pool and said, "Let me first start by saying that there has never been a case of one person ridin' the coattails of two other people like the way I did here tonight."

❖

By the end of the off-season, as the Comets' season drew nearer, people started to take notice of what Van was doing out in the community, and the crowds were huge everywhere we went. I no longer had to call on blind lists, as people were now calling me to have Van come speak at their functions. We sold a lot of season tickets right on the spot, and the crowds at Comets games got considerably bigger the second season. But the long WNBA off-season had taken its toll on Van and he couldn't wait to get going again. By the time April rolled around, he told me that he needed to slow down on the appearances and concentrate on basketball.

Besides that, Van had another interest at home that was far more important than basketball. In August 1997, as the inaugural season was winding down, Van and Betty were blessed with their first grandchild, Nicholas. Van's daughter, Renee, gave birth to Nicholas on August 13, 1997 and he's been a load of fun for Van and Betty ever since. That little guy followed Van everywhere during the off-season and he's been by Van's side ever since. Van can't go far today without Nicholas making a fuss about going with him. There were many days at Westside during practice when Van showed up with a proud look on his face and a grandson on his arm.

Van's done a lot of interviews for a lot of different news organizations since taking the Houston position, but none was as good as the piece on Nicholas and him done by NBA Entertainment. The piece ran on *NBA Inside Stuff* and it put a lump in Van's throat when he saw it for the first time. The crew showed up at my office at 2 Greenway in the morning and we headed to Van's house. I told Van about the piece a week before the NBA Entertainment guys got to Houston, but he failed to tell Betty. I was in the car with Van and Betty the day before the shoot was to take place, and reminded him about it. "Oh yeah, I forgot to tell ya' that we're going to have some people over to the house tomorrow doing an interview," he said to Betty who was in the back seat. There was no response from Betty for a good minute and I could sense the tension in the car.

"I'm guessing by your silence that I'm in a little trouble," Van said. "Well Good Lord, Van, at least you could have told me so I can get the house ready for company," Betty said with disgust in her voice. "Well what do you think I'm doing now? They're not going to be there until tomorrow," Van responded. When I showed up the next day with the NBA crew, the house had been de-Nicholasized—all signs of a toddler were gone and the house was spotless.

It didn't take long for all Betty's hard work to be nullified as Van began playing with Nick. The crew spent most of the day at their house and it turned out to be a great story because Nick was at such a fun time in his life; he was just learning to crawl up and down the stairs, walk, and really mess around. The two had a lot of fun that day and the

NBA Entertainment crew really captured the love Van has for him.

Van feels some guilt over spending so much time with his grandchildren when he didn't spend the same type of quality time with his own children. He was always so wrapped up in Ole Miss basketball that he missed a lot of his children's growing up. Van's commented to Betty on several occasions about Nicholas' progress, and how astonished he was when Nick began to walk, run, talk, and do a lot of other things. Betty's often said to him, "You know, Van, our kids did the same thing but you were just too busy to notice." He regrets that, but he knows that his children understand the love he has for them, and he feels like he's been given a second chance as a grandfather.

While Van was still coaching in high school, there were a few times when Betty had to leave home and Van was responsible for babysitting the two children. Needless to say, Van's interest in babysitting at the time was limited, especially in the middle of the basketball season. Van's said countless times, "If it can't help me win basketball games, don't bring it up." Babysitting was a distraction. It didn't happen often during his coaching career while the children were young, but occasionally he had to watch Johnny and Renee during practice. He had no choice—he had to overcome some obstacles in order to get in a good practice, so he tied Johnny and Renee's walkers to the basket stanchion for the two-hour practice. He can laugh about it now, but thirty years ago I'm sure it raised an eyebrow or two for anyone who sat and watched his practice.

As the Comets started the second season in defense of their WNBA title, Nicholas was at a lot of the practices, and not once was he tied to the basket stanchion at Westside. But that was the least of Van's concerns. He knew he had some issues as they entered the second season. Actually,

Van couldn't wait to get started and he couldn't wait to face these potential problems so he knew where he stood. Everyone he knew told him about the problems he was going to have now that Sheryl Swoopes was healthy and would be able to play the entire season. I think Van was the only one on the planet who didn't see this as that big a problem.

In one of the most-documented pregnancies in women's athletics, Sheryl gave birth to Jordan in June 1997 and had to miss a significant amount of the first season. The fact that she even returned to Houston's lineup that season astonished everyone in the sports world and created more media interest than anything else the first year. She gave birth to Jordan on June 25 and returned for a home game against Phoenix on August 7—just six weeks between labor and lay-ups.

Sheryl worked hard during the off-season to get herself ready for the second season. Van kept a close eye on her progress and was excited about having such a pure shooter in his lineup. While everyone told him about his impending problems, Van saw limitless opportunities. After Jordan was born, Sheryl didn't waste any time in finding out from her doctors when she could rejoin her team and start playing again. She went full throttle from the time Jordan took his first breath until she finally got her legs under her and was competing again.

She was ready to go when camp opened in the spring of 1998 and she looked like a different person when she arrived at camp. She was in great shape, she was quick and she could still shoot. A lot of people thought Van had his hands full with Sheryl, Cynthia Cooper and Tina Thompson on the floor at the same time because there wouldn't be enough shots to go around. Van won't deny that it did concern him, but he thought more about the possibilities of having a great team and a chance at repeating. When he thought about his situation, he didn't see it as not having enough shots, he thought about having two of the greatest shooters in the game on each wing and having the most dominant post-player in the game on the floor at the same time. He was excited and anxious, not worried.

To no one's surprise, it didn't go perfectly and the team did have some problems as they got ready for the 1998 season. No successful team goes through an entire season without a few issues, but the Comets worked through them and every WNBA team that tried to throw something at them found it out quickly. The Comets were good—incredibly good that year. They finished the regular season at 27-3 and Van told me that the three losses kind of surprised him. He felt every time they took the floor that they had the better team and the better talent and he expected to win—every time. The phantom problems between Sheryl and Cynthia were well documented all season. From media day to the start of the season, to our championship parade, the media was looking for something between those two. If Sheryl sneezed and Cynthia didn't say, "Bless you," they wanted to make something of it. Tina Thompson expressed it best when she said, "Look, we're not a bunch of Girl Scouts out there. We're not always going to be best friends. As long as we get along for forty minutes each night."

But the media and a lot of people who thought they were close to the team didn't see what Van and the rest of the team saw every day in practice. Tina was right, they didn't have to be best friends, they just had to play together, and when the five starters were all on the same page they were nearly unbeatable. Both Cynthia and Sheryl are great passers and a lot of that was overlooked the entire season because everyone was so hung up on the number of shots each one got. The media didn't get to see the high-fives, the "Nice pass" comments, and the respect they had for each other on the floor.

Thankfully the *Houston Chronicle* beat writer, William

Stickney, or 'Stick,' was fair, and the majority of the coverage about the Comets was positive. Van has become great friends with Stick over the last three years, and he really looks forward to seeing him at practice and at games both on the road and at home. It's not often that you find someone you immediately become close friends with, but with Van and Stick it's been that way from day one. Plus, he's the team's beat writer, so I was really pleased when the two of them hit it off. If there's ever one guy you want your head coach to become buddies with, it's the team's beat writer at the paper. It was a lot of other media from around the country that caused the Comets so much grief about the Cynthia and Sheryl situation. Every day, every game, they were looking for something new.

Sheryl collapsed at a practice the day before a nationally televised game. We later found out that she just needed to change her eating habits, but at the time of the collapse it was one of the scariest things Van and the rest of the audience at practice had ever witnessed. She went down like a rock under the west basket at Westside. It was at the end of practice, and some players were just shooting around and some were in the training room getting treatment. When Sheryl went down, Cynthia was the furthest away from the incident and the first one to her side. A lot of us stood around and looked at Sheryl as she began to convulse on the floor, but Cynthia sprinted from the training room and put Sheryl in her arms, trying to wake her.

"With as many things going on in my head at that moment, the one that stood out was the respect Cynthia had for another great athlete and a fellow human being," Van said.

Following our second championship parade in downtown Houston, a media person asked Van what he was going to do about the problems between Cynthia and Sheryl in the upcoming off-season. "We were 27-3 and just won our second straight WNBA championship," Van replied with disgust. "What more do you want? If this is a problem, I'll take it every day."

❖

The Comets entered the season with high hopes in 1998 with the thought of defending their inaugural season championship. It seemed everybody associated with the WNBA thought the Comets would struggle because they had too much talent and not enough basketballs to go around. It didn't take long for Van to shut everybody up. Houston was solid from game one to game thirty and during that time put together a streak of fifteen straight wins—the longest in WNBA history.

During the course of the 1998 season, Van never realized what they had accomplished until the season was over and he had a chance to look back. Travel in the WNBA is incredibly difficult and WNBA teams play a lot of games in a short amount of time. To go 27-3 and win 90 percent of the games under those circumstances is really incredible.

There were many back-to-back situations, and they played three games in four nights more than once. Unlike the NBA, WNBA teams don't travel on chartered flights. They fly commercially, and Houston, along with every other team in the WNBA, had their share of layovers, all-day travel, and basic traveling headaches.

"When I look back at what we did in 1998, I realize that it was a once in a lifetime situation and that we set a standard in women's professional basketball," Van said. "The fifteen-game winning streak, under the conditions in which we did it almost amazes me more than the 27-3 record. We didn't lose a game for a long time, and after a while I just expected us to win every time we took the floor."

Houston got off to a quick start, winning their first five games. In the midst of the winning streak the Comets were in Los Angeles for a big Western Conference match-up. The Sparks were 2-2 at the time and Houston was 4-0 and had already taken a two-game lead over Los Angeles. Before the game, Van put together one of his "Pre-game speeches for the Ages" and was fired-up in the locker room.

"I feel good, gang, really good," he said clapping his hands and walking back and forth in front of his players. "I need rebounds tonight, gang. They're a lot bigger than us." Walking toward starting center Monica Lamb, Van said, "Monica, tonight, your nickname is Monica, Mojo, rebounding machine, Lamb—okay?" She responded with a double double of fourteen points and eleven rebounds.

Houston's first loss came in Phoenix to the Mercury on June 24. But the Comets redeemed themselves later in the season with a win at America West Arena on July 21. Ironically, following the July 21 game, Phoenix coach Cheryl Miller grabbed the public address microphone, stood in the middle of the floor and announced to the frenzied Mercury crowd, "Don't worry Mercury fans. I know we lost tonight, but what you saw here was a preview to the WNBA championship. And when it comes around, we're going to win that bad boy!"

Van was in the locker room and came out into the hallway when he heard the crowd. He knew something was up because they'd just gotten beat, so he couldn't understand why the crowd was so loud. As he listened to Cheryl Miller, he thought it was incredibly bold on her part to make that prediction, but as it turns out she got the part about it being a preview to the WNBA championship right. It was the tail end of her statement where Van thought they could make a little adjustment.

In the midst of Houston's streak of fifteen straight wins, Van realized that they had a chance of doing something special that season. They were 20-1 with nine games to play and they were undefeated at home. Van wasn't sure they could win the rest of their games and finish at 29-1, but it was now a realistic goal to not lose another game at Compaq

Center. Van didn't want to let the Houston fans down; he felt they were as caught up in the team as he was and he didn't want to let anyone down at home.

But the Cleveland Rockers snapped the fifteen-game winning streak in overtime at home on August 1. The loss bothered Van and he couldn't understand why his team couldn't take advantage of their home floor. Obviously, every team is going to lose some games, but after starting 20-1, Van was confident they could stay perfect at home. Actually, they were in rather good shape in the Cleveland game but fell apart down the stretch. But they regrouped and finished strong and went 7-1 the rest of the way and again secured the number one seed in the WNBA playoffs.

"At one point late in the season, I looked at our box score from the August 10 game against Charlotte and our record read 25-2," Van said. "It was hard to believe, but I also knew at that point that we had a real chance of repeating. I knew we had the best players in the league and that we couldn't be stopped if we were hitting all cylinders."

Houston's other loss down the stretch came at New York, when the Liberty really pounded them at Madison Square Garden. The Comets had already secured the number one seed in the playoffs when they went to New York. They had actually secured home court for many weeks before they ever traveled there. The Liberty, however, were fighting for a playoff spot and needed a win desperately. They got one, but didn't get another the rest of the season and failed to qualify for the post-season. They got up for the Comets that day, but after defeating them they never regained their fire.

That's something Houston battled all season long: they were the defending champions, they were rolling through their regular-season schedule and every one was gunning for them. That makes the 27-3 mark even more impressive for Van, knowing that every team brought a solid effort every time they took the floor against his team. Houston was at Washington late in the season when the Mystics were clearly out of the playoff picture. They entered the game with a 3-26 mark, but when they hosted the Comets on August 17, the building was packed and Washington played with a lot of energy—it was their championship game. But Van always had his crew ready and they rose to the challenge. In Washington, they scored 110 points—a WNBA record.

Just as in the 1997 season, Houston played the Charlotte Sting in the first round of the playoffs. Unlike the '97 season, the league went to a multiple-game format rather than a single-elimination post-season. The format was now best two-out-of-three to advance to the next round. Van didn't mind the new format because he felt the better team had a chance of advancing in a three-game series rather than a one-game shootout. However, he didn't like the fact that the higher-seeded team was on the road for the first game before returning home for games two and three.

It meant that the Comets had to go to Charlotte for game one of their semifinal series. A loss at Charlotte would put Houston in a real bind before coming home to Compaq Center, where they would face elimination. It didn't seem fair to Van that the higher-seeded team opened on the road. I'm sure he'd have a lot of supporters in Cleveland, as the Rockers were the number two seed and should have played host to the lower-seeded Phoenix Mercury in game one of their semifinal series. But the Rockers had to go to Phoenix to open the series. They lost game one and were in the tough situation of being one game away from elimination without even having played a home game yet. Cleveland eventually lost the series to Phoenix, and that was the fear Van had about the format.

Fortunately, Houston played really well against Charlotte and swept the Sting, 2-0. They were now at a point in the season where they had a chance to defend their title as they faced the Phoenix Mercury in the WNBA championship. Van was stunned that they were facing Phoenix in the finals. One day on the bus just before the playoffs started, Van got a group of us together and we made predictions on how we thought the playoffs would shake out. Not a single person had Phoenix in the finals; a number of us didn't have them even making the post-season.

But they came on strong down the stretch and were obviously playing well to defeat Cleveland in the semifinals. After winning game one against the Rockers in Phoenix, they lost game two in Cleveland but won game three at Gund Arena, home of the Rockers. Van knew they were playing well and the thought of opening the series at hostile America West Arena scared him. He thought a fair format would have been game one in Houston, game two in Phoenix and game three back in Houston. It upset Van because he knew he had the best team with the best record and was the number one seed, yet they started the championship series in Phoenix.

Game one against the Mercury was a war. America West Arena was deafening, probably one of the loudest games I've ever heard. It went back and forth for most of the game and fittingly was a nail-biter into the final minutes. The game was tied at 51 with a little over a minute to play. Houston had a couple of good looks at the basket but they couldn't convert and Phoenix called time out with thirty-three seconds left.

The Comets had dominated most of their competition for much of the year, but Van knew this game would be close. They had crushed teams in the early parts of games and cruised to victory in the second half. Earlier in the year, Houston had New York down 42-12 at Madison Square

Garden in their first meeting of the season, and it wasn't uncommon for them to bury teams right away.

But when they didn't run away from Phoenix at the start, Van knew it was going to be a struggle for forty minutes. Van felt he made some coaching mistakes throughout that game and he felt a sense of relief that they were still in a position to steal game one with the game tied. With less than twenty seconds to play, the Mercury worked the clock and finally got the ball down to one of the great post players in the WNBA, Jennifer Gillom. Van's always said that she was clearly one of the best players in the league after having such a great college coach.

She turned and scored with eight seconds to play and it sounded like a bomb going off in America West Arena when the crowd exploded. It was so strange as the Mercury set up their offense—it seemed almost dead quiet in the arena. But when Gillom hit the turnaround, it was deafening.

Van called timeout and was angry with himself. He felt he should have doubled Gillom on that final play, but he didn't see it coming and he didn't instruct his players to look for it. Phoenix hadn't run her in the low post the entire game, but Van still felt he should have seen it coming on a big play like that so late in the game. They ran her in the low post and he didn't have anyone help Tina Thompson, who was guarding her. He thought he should have had Sheryl Swoopes or Kim Perrot double Gillom if she got the ball in the low post. She got the ball, he didn't double her and it cost them the game down the stretch.

That really gnawed at Van, feeling that he'd blown the first game and now his team was in a dramatic hole. When the game was over and the media came into our locker room, several of them asked Van how he thought his team would react being down 1-0 to Phoenix and facing elimination when the series returned to Houston. He gave them the canned answer, but they kept harping on the fact that they thought the Comets were still relaxed after the game and didn't seemed concerned about the loss.

"They kept asking me that and I didn't know how to answer about how our players were feeling. But don't kid yourselves, we were concerned," he said. "We were down 1-0 and were just one game away from ending our season as the runner-up after going 27-3 in the regular season. All Phoenix had to do now was steal one of two games at Compaq Center and our incredible season would have been an incredible disappointment."

Van has said that he made some other decisions he didn't like during that game. He second-guessed himself the entire forty minutes and he knew he'd made some mistakes throughout the night. He felt a real sense of responsibility for the game one defeat in Phoenix.

"Our players had busted their butts, not only for forty minutes that night but for an entire season, and now I felt like I'd put us in a tough position because of my poor judgement," he said. "I've let a lot of games bother me in my coaching career, but that one certainly stands out."

After the game the coaching staff walked back to the hotel, which was located in downtown Phoenix, not far from America West Arena. As I walked with the frustrated staff, someone had the guts to ask if we were going to grab a bite to eat at Dan Majerle's Restaurant before we called it a night and went back to our rooms.

"Let me tell you something right now gang, you may get a chance to eat sometime next week, but right now you're all going back to the room with me to figure out some way to beat Phoenix," Van told them before any of them had any illusions about eating. He finally let them get some room service deep into the night, but by that time he knew he had their attention and that he was taking this whole Phoenix Mercury thing pretty seriously.

The Comets came back to Houston for game two and Van couldn't believe the media attention surrounding this series. In some markets the WNBA has taken off and grown faster than anyone would have ever guessed. Houston is one of those cities, and when the Comets returned home the media was all over the place waiting to talk to Van after our first practice at Compaq Center. When they finally got done with practice, the media people came onto the floor and Van, Cynthia, Sheryl and Tina were drilled with question after question. Although Van would rather have been in a different situation, he loved the fact that the media and the entire city of Houston were focused on the championship series.

When he left the floor and the Mercury were coming out of their locker room for practice, Van crossed paths with Jennifer Gillom and said, "Jen, I don't care who beats me tomorrow, but it ain't gonna be you."

❖

Van's never known a more hopeless feeling as a coach than he did on Saturday, August 29, 1998—the night of the second game of the WNBA Finals. They went 27-3 in the regular season, blew past Charlotte in the semifinals and were now looking to get swept in the finals by Phoenix—a team that Van didn't even think would make the playoffs.

Phoenix outplayed the Comets for nearly the entire game and Van and crew found themselves down twelve points with a little over seven minutes to play. Van, along with 16,285 other Comets fans in the building, knew there was no chance of catching them. When Michele Timms hit a free throw with 7:24 remaining to give the Mercury their biggest lead in the game at 62-50, Van sat down on the bench and felt like somebody just knocked him up along side the head with a 2 x 4. I made eye contact with him when he looked down press row and Stick and I were looking back with anxious eyes. He looked the other way and saw a handful of Comets players on the bench with an absolute helpless looks on their faces.

How the Comets came back that night is still up for discussion. Phoenix absolutely beat them to every loose ball, out-shot them, out-rebounded them, and just flat outplayed Houston. They led 37-32 at halftime and Van was concerned even at that point because he knew they were being outplayed on every inch of the Compaq Center floor.

It didn't get better in the second half as the Mercury beat Houston in every aspect of the game for the first thirteen minutes of the half. But after Timms made her free throw, Van called a memorable timeout, hoping to put together one last little miracle. I'll never forget Kim Perrot during that timeout: she was all over the players in the huddle, telling them that they had time, that they could do it, and that they had to make plays and play better defense.

During the timeout, I noticed the Compaq Center security guards taking positions around the court, and I saw WNBA president Val Ackerman with Mark Pray, the league's director of public relations. They, along with other WNBA officials, were getting ready for the awards ceremony that was sure to take place in just a few minutes. Van dropped his head, thought for a moment, and looked back up at his players.

"See that?" he told his players as he pointed to the WNBA officials standing near the Comets' bench with the WNBA Championship trophy in hand. "They're getting ready to give Phoenix that championship trophy. Are you gonna let that happen? Are you gonna let those players celebrate a WNBA championship on your floor? That's your trophy. It belongs here. You've earned it. Don't let it happen."

It was as if reality had started setting in on Houston and the sense of urgency began to gnaw at them. This was it. Despite the incredible record throughout the three months of the WNBA season, Van was minutes away from having the worst feeling in all of sports—losing your final game of the season.

In the final minutes Houston outscored Phoenix 16-4 in one of the most amazing comebacks I've ever witnessed. The Comets actually took the lead with 1:25 to play when Cooper hit a huge three-pointer to put them up 66-64. The Mercury's Kristi Harrower scored with exactly one minute to play, which tied the game at 66. Houston had a good look at the basket with less than thirty seconds to play, but I've never seen a bunch of players so tight in all my life. Houston's best bet at this point was to get it into overtime, where Van thought they would have a good shot at winning. It almost didn't get to overtime as Phoenix got the ball back and Timms' three-pointer at the buzzer looked good for a moment, but bounced off the rim as the horn sounded.

"When that baby was in the air, it looked good and I thought to myself, 'well at least Jennifer Gillom didn't beat me,'" Van said. "Actually, I looked up and saw that we didn't have anybody under the basket and I was scared to death they were going to get an easy put-back as the buzzer sounded. When she shot it I was hoping it was the highest-arcing shot in the history of basketball because I wanted time to run out. I can't imagine getting beat on a put-back as time expired."

Houston scored first in overtime and never trailed again, winning 74-69. Van told his team before the start of the extra period that they had to double- and triple-team Jennifer Gillom. He was determined not to lose to Phoenix in overtime the way they did in game one. Van doesn't show a lot of emotion after a win, but after seemingly coming back from the dead and winning game two, Van raised his fist in the air and was incredibly excited on the floor before he made it back to the locker room. After he sat there room for a few minutes, he began to think back about the game and he scared himself thinking of how close he'd come to letting his team down by not putting them in a position to win. The next nine months would have been the longest in Van's life if they hadn't pulled out that miracle against Phoenix.

Although Van was grateful for the game two victory he was smart enough to realize that something was wrong with the offense. He knew he had to tweak it a bit for game three because they just weren't the scoring force against Phoenix in the finals that they were during the regular season. A phone call from his old friend Richard Williams—the former Mississippi State men's head coach, who coached the Bulldogs from 1986–1998-got Van thinking about the motion in his team's offense, and he had a new game plan for the Comets after that conversation. Anyone who knows Van knows that he diagrams plays on anything he can get his hands on. On the airplane, at the dinner table, or even driving down I-45 in the middle of Houston, Van's always diagramming new plays and new sets for his team. If you're ever in a meeting with him it's best to keep everything close or you'll go back to the office only to find an important document covered from top to bottom with flex offenses and trapping defenses. After Van talked with Richard Williams, he was on a rampage diagramming a new offense for game three.

The morning following game two, Van went to church with Betty, and he spent the entire sermon diagramming on the church bulletin. He couldn't help it; he tried his best to listen to what the preacher was saying but he just couldn't get his mind off of this new offense and how he was going to convince his team to accept it for this important game. He knew he had to get to church on Sunday. He's always said, "The good Lord helps those people who help themselves," and there was no doubt in his mind that the Lord helped him win game two.

"I felt like the Lord was saying, 'Son listen, I helped you get this second game, now you better find yourself a way to win this third one. I've done helped you enough.'" I'm not saying that's exactly the right way to look at things, but that's exactly how I felt."

After church Van headed to Westside and spent the entire day in his office looking for ways to improve the offense. He didn't want to leave a single stone unturned making sure he was totally prepared for game three. He felt like they got a second chance after the miracle of game two and he didn't want to let it slip away now.

❖

When Monday's practice finally rolled around, Van knew he had to sell his players on this new offense that he wanted to implement. The team got together in the locker room prior to taking the floor, and Van grabbed a white PowerAde towel off the ball rack. He held the towel up and asked the players what color they thought the towel was. It was quite obvious the towel was white and because of the nature of the question, he didn't get any response.

"C'mon, gang, what color is this towel?" he asked again.

"Looks to be an off-white," Kim Perrot said.

"You're obviously up to something, so I'm gonna say that it's anything but white," Cooper said.

Van began to drop hundred-dollar bills on the floor of the locker room, which got the attention of every person in the room.

"If you believe in what I'm gonna try and tell 'ya, then we're each gonna win a championship and each one of you is gonna pick up $10 thousand," Van told them. "So beginning today, no matter what I say, just believe in it. Okay?"

"Coach, uh, what does that money on the floor and you asking us to believe in everything you say have to do with that white towel?" Cynthia asked.

"If I tell you this towel is purple, then it's purple. Do you believe me that's it's purple?" Van asked.

"So you're telling me that if we believe in everything you have to say over the next two days, then we're gonna win another WNBA championship. If that's the case, then I got just one question for you," Cynthia said. "Is that towel a light purple or a dark purple?"

Van knew it was going to be difficult to convince his team to change their offense this deep into the season, but at least now he knew he had a start when Cynthia said that. Van was obviously taking game three and this championship seriously. After he finished with his purple towel demonstration, he went into a serious talk. His voice level rose and he had a lot of instructions on what he thought went wrong. Throughout my two seasons with Van he never once closed our locker room to the national media for a pre-game or post-game talk, but he wanted to make that change for game three because he felt there were too many distractions for his team. It was also one of the few times that I ever heard Van swear—okay, kind of swear.

"Tom, I want to have this locker room closed at all times unless it's a mandated time for the media," he said to me while the entire team was still sitting in the locker room. I didn't care what he said; my eyes were transfixed by the hundred-dollar bills on the floor at his feet. "And I don't want anybody in here for the pre-game—NBC, NBA Entertainment, nobody. If the league doesn't like it, they can just kiss my a— butt!"

"Sounds good," I replied. I wasn't going to argue with him, but I still wanted to make sure he fully realized what he was saying. "However, Van, if you—"

"I don't give a rippin' flippin' double-damn," Van said and he stormed out of the locker room. Cynthia looked at me with the strangest look on her face, as if to say, "Did he just say rippin' flippin double-damn?"

The team left the locker room and made it to the floor, where they worked on the new offense and Van took a lot of the players aside and explained it to them. When it was time for game three Van felt comfortable with his situation and thought it was the first time in the series against Phoenix that the players looked relaxed and confident.

During the first two seasons the Comets always ended practice with a half-court challenge. It was always a big-time event and Van always participated. During the 1998 playoffs the team was so high-strung and intense that the half-court shots began to taper off. When the team was breaking up after learning the new offense, each player went her separate way. Jim Kozimor, Houston's play-by-play announcer, suggested to Van that he should have everybody participate in the half-court shot to loosen everyone up. They ran through the contest and it was the first time during the entire series that I saw everyone associated with the team laugh.

The Compaq Center was electrifying again for game three. When the Comets made their way out of the locker room and onto the court for the first time, a bunch of Comets fans got confused looks on their faces when Van and the coaching staff sat down with purple towels in hand. But Van loved it. Every towel they used that day was a deep, dark purple. He had to make some adjustments during the game and he needed his players to believe in what he was doing; the purple towels all over the bench for forty minutes helped him make the point.

The Comets were in control the entire game and Van was confident from the opening tip that they would win. It was an amazing accomplishment for the players, the front office, and the entire city of Houston. I've never been around a community as big as Houston that had such loyal fans and supported its team's every move. When the final buzzer sounded and we had our second group hug in as many years, I thought back to the start of this whole thing and I knew it was the highlight of my professional career.

By this time in their franchise history the Comets had become incredibly popular in Houston. There weren't very many sports fans in the city who didn't know who they were now. We went with the safe route after winning the first championship by having the celebration on the steps of City Hall. The second year, we blew it out and had a parade through the streets of downtown Houston. Van was one of the bigger supporters of the parade and he also felt the city was ready for a Comets Championship Parade.

"Let's get going on a parade, boy," Van said hours after we won game three. "I mean I can understand what we did last year but don't you think this city is ready for a parade? I can't believe we wouldn't get a great crowd to come out. Did you hear that place today?"

He was right. The city was ready to see the Comets strut their stuff through Houston. Just two days after winning their second title in as many years, Van, his team and members of the front office staff jumped on five Houston fire engines and went down the same route the Rockets had taken just three years earlier. It was estimated that nearly 100,000 people came out to see the Comets through the streets of Houston. Indeed, we'd come a long way from a church basement with stale cookies and orange soda.

Van had a great time that day and did his best to shake all 100,000 hands. He had Nicholas on his lap, and the two waved to as many as they could. The parade ended and the team was driving to City Hall again for another rally.

"Y'all getting' used to this yet?' Van said from the podium to the horde of screaming fans, which had grown dramatically over last year's crowd. It seemed that most of the 100,000 who lined the streets did all they could to cram into the area near the reflecting pool outside City Hall. And for the second straight year, Van said all the right things. "We didn't have a prayer to win game two against Phoenix, right? I can only think of one thing that got us through when we were down twelve with seven minutes to play—you!"

Van looks back now on the 1998 season with great memories. Fans don't like to compare the WNBA to the NBA game, but what Houston accomplished in 1998 is truly remarkable. The Comets won 90 percent of their games—more than any other professional basketball team in the United States, men or women. The 1995–96 Chicago Bulls won 87.8 percent of their games when they went 72-10—the best finish in NBA history.

Van had every reason to be proud of his accomplishments after two seasons. His team had won two WNBA championships and gone 51-14 over the course of two years. But even more impressive for Van was the fact that eighteen months earlier, the franchise was nonexistent. He's proud of that the most.

The Comets went through some changes following the second season. I left for the Los Angeles Lakers and Jim Kozimor left for the Sacramento Kings and Monarchs. But more importantly, Van had to get ready for a season without Peggie by his side for the first time in twenty years. Alisa Scott joined the team midway through the 1998 season when Peggie left for Texas A & M, so Van had an assistant in place, but now he was faced with breaking in a new coaching staff as they prepared for a season.

The first two years were a magical time, a time that I know will stay with me forever. We could win 20 WNBA championships and it would be tough to imagine they could be any better than the first two. I didn't know it at the time, but Game 3 was the last game that Kim Perrot would ever play, and without Kim on our roster, the magic of the first two seasons would never be recaptured.

❖

Post Game Press Conference
Game 3, WNBA Finals, September 1, 1998

Van's opening remarks: "Let me tell you right now: Look out golf courses, look out Astros baseball, Ole Miss, Rice and Texas A & M football because I'm going to enjoy relaxing. My goal is to play every free round of golf from now until the next basketball season. Was that a game? Yes, it was. If you're from Phoenix you ought to really be proud of that team. They did a marvelous job. They played some great basketball. I thought it was one of the best games I've seen. And I'm so proud we won our second championship in a row. Thank God for great players."

Q: "Down the stretch, both teams were trading baskets. What did your team do better?"

Van: "During a timeout, I told them that we needed to guard someone. We made a defensive adjustment. We allowed them to go down the middle and so we told them to push them down the sidelines, cut a few passing lanes, step it up defensively. That's when we won the game—with a gallant, valiant effort by Kim Perrot. She's had two bad games and that's unbelievable. The Big Three are going to get all of the publicity, but poor old Kim is always there. I told her, 'Kim, just get me one rebound.' And she got me three among all those giants. That's coaching right there. That's listening, I didn't ask for but one."

Chapter 11
An Unforgettable Friend

JUST LIKE AFTER OUR FIRST SEASON, it was our plan to build on our momentum and make the Comets bigger than the year before. The season before seemed to be a success when Van made all of his speaking, radio and television appearances. We wanted to duplicate it and I talked with Van about it following the second championship. He agreed. We needed to continue the momentum but he wanted to go about it differently.

Rather than go out and make appearances, he wanted to help out one of his players, Kim Perrot. Although Kim had been vital to winning the first two championships and was the heart and soul of those teams, she still earned the league minimum. She'd signed with the Comets as a developmental player in 1997 and couldn't make more than the minimum the first season. She got a little more in 1998, but certainly not enough to validate her contribution to the championships and not enough to live on for the entire off-season.

Van met with CD and told him that he wanted the Comets to hire Kim during the off-season to be a spokesperson for the team. Van did it for free a year earlier, but he made a case for Kim; he wanted her to be taken care of because he knew all that she'd done for him in helping win the first two titles.

The Comets hired Kim, and I worked with her the same way I had with Van the previous year. I scheduled her for as many appearances as I could because, after the second championship, the Comets were red-hot in the city of Houston and she was incredibly popular. During the first season Kim bent my ear on several occasions about the replica jerseys we sold throughout Houston, and the fact that none of them were replicas of her Number 10. We had Cynthia Cooper, Sheryl Swoopes, Tina Thompson and Wanda Guyton jerseys, but zero Kim Perrot's.

"I'm telling ya, Tom. I live in Houston and I got a lot of fans," she told me. "You guys make some Number 10 jerseys and stick them in the Rockets Shop and I guarantee you they'll sell."

"Guarantee it, huh?" I said.

"You think I'm kidding?" she asked. "You try it, you'll see." She was right, we had Kim Perrot jerseys made and put into stores all over Houston and they sold as fast as any jersey we had—Comets or Rockets.

Van, Kim, CD and I all met at Westside after she was hired, We told her what we hoped she could accomplish; she was very excited about the possibilities and was ready to go from day one. After the meeting, Van pulled her aside and told her to do everything I asked her to do, but warned that she should expect to be lost more than not. I didn't care what he said; I was just happy to be traveling with somebody this year who was from Houston and could keep us on the right path.

We started in October, hitting as many civic clubs, schools, churches and autograph sessions as we could. From day one we had people calling us for appearances, and very rarely did I get into a jam where we didn't have any appearances scheduled and I had to make calls. On the Monday before Thanksgiving, Kim met with Van and me at Westside.

"I'd like to do something for Thanksgiving," Kim said.

"Something for the people of Houston; I don't know, some sort of a 'Kim Perrot Foundation' that we can do for the underprivileged of Houston."

"That's great, Kimbo, but Thanksgiving is three days away. Don't you think it may be a little late to be putting together a foundation?" Van said.

We never did put together a Thanksgiving Foundation with Kim's name on it. But after the holiday break I asked her what she did for Thanksgiving. She told me she went to a shelter in Houston and helped serve dinner to thousands of Houstonians in need. That was the kind of person she was; it's no wonder she and Van became so close during her two years with the Comets.

With all the problems they had on the court, I've never seen a coach and player become closer off the court than Van and Kim. Van admittedly coached her worse than any other player he'd coached before, but she always stayed loyal to him. Every time I was around the two of them they were joking, laughing, playing cards or dominos and enjoying each other's company.

Despite their shaky beginnings they grew to become a dynamic tandem on the court. Van finally realized Kim's value to the team midway through the first season, when he was still giving her spotty minutes, jerking her in and out of the game every time any little thing went awry. Following practice one day at Westside, Van picked up his mail—at that time neither he nor anyone else on the team was getting any fan mail. So when Van got an envelope addressed to him that looked like it could be from a fan, he opened it immediately. It read: "Van, players like Kim Perrot are one-in-a-million. You need to realize that coaches like you are a dime-a-dozen, and we're not afraid to write Les Alexander and tell him the exact same thing." Van called Kim into his office and told her that he was beginning to see the light as he showed her the letter. From that point on the friendship really began to grow.

One night after a game in Detroit during the 1998 season, we defeated the Shock and then headed to Champp's Sports Café—right across the street from our hotel. Van, Kim and I walked over to the restaurant and I couldn't get a word in, no matter how hard I tried. The two of them talked about the game and kidded around like they'd been best friends forever.

"You know, Tom," Kim said as we ate a late dinner, "I sure have grown fond of this old boy from Mississippi."

Kim and I continued our appearances at a feverish pace and finally took a break for the Christmas holiday. When I returned from our break I informed Kim that I would be leaving the Comets for a new position with the Lakers, but that the new PR director of the team, Megan Bonifas, would continue working with her on the appearances. I left for Los Angeles on January 24, and when I left Kim she was the picture of health. On February 21, just four weeks after leaving Houston, I was in a bus in Denver with the Lakers heading to the airport late at night when my cellular phone rang. It was Tim Frank, the PR director for the Rockets, who informed me that Kim had been diagnosed with lung and brain cancer. I was stunned, and couldn't wait to get off the bus that night to collect my thoughts.

Obviously it shook me, but not nearly as hard as it did Van. He didn't have a clue that she was even feeling sick, and as far as he knew she was making appearances for the Comets and staying in shape for the upcoming season. It wasn't uncommon for her to spend ten to twelve hours a day playing basketball at a local gymnasium in Houston and Van continually checked on her game throughout the off-season. But one day in early February, while working out with some of the strength and conditioning coaches at Westside, Kim began to feel dizzy and felt numbness in her face. The team's trainer, Michele Leget, had her visit team doctors and on February 19, 1999 they gave her the horrifying diagnosis. On August 19, 1999 Kim died of cancer.

In just six short months, Kim went from a world-class athlete and one of the best point guards in the WNBA, to a cancer patient who lost her bout to the dreaded disease. Kim's death shook Van to the core and hurt everyone associated with the team. The Comets were in Los Angeles on the day she died, as they were scheduled to play the Sparks the following night. A night earlier Van was with Kim at a Houston hospital until midnight, and he knew it wouldn't be long until she was gone. He just didn't realize it would be the next day.

For a team that was continually being blamed for not being together, not being a close-knit bunch, you should have seen them on August 19 when they got the news of Kim's death. The team gathered in Van's hotel room in Los Angeles and cried, talked, and prayed together. The Los Angeles Lakers' chaplain, Frank Harville, came to the team's hotel and led them in a half-hour chapel to help make sense of this tragedy. After Frank left, Van stood up and talked to his team for a moment.

"I know my words are going to be shallow because everyone has their own special memories of Kim," he said. "Yes, it's terribly sad that Kim is gone and I know that I'll never get another chance to play dominos with her or have another chance to see her play basketball again. But I'm grateful that my life and hers crossed paths. Although it was just two-and-a-half years I got to know Kim, they were two-and-a-half very special years."

Van fought back a lot of tears that day in the Los Angeles Marriott, but he wasn't alone. That was an incredibly long day for the Comets and everyone associated with the team.

❖

Van was golfing with Kevin Cook back in February when

CD called him and gave him the news of Kim's diagnosis. He left the golf course immediately and began to face this horrible reality. Van just couldn't believe that this young person, an incredible athlete who had helped lead his team to a WNBA championship just four months earlier was now going to have to fight for her life.

He left the course in such a rush, such a confusing, horrified state. He and Kevin got to the parking lot, threw everything in the trunk and in the back seat of Van's car. In the confusion, Van locked his keys in the trunk and the two had to wait for assistance. He was so derailed and confused just then. It was a surreal moment—one of those when time seemed to stand still and every thought, every word, every movement was in slow motion.

The team held a press conference a few weeks later to announce Kim's diagnosis; it was the toughest press conference Van's ever had. Kim had become incredibly popular in Houston with her charitable work, and her fans needed to know what kind of fight she was up against. Kim began to cry at the press conference when she made the announcement, and Van was unable to fight off tears. When it was time for him to comment he was unable to say a word. He sat there with his hands in his face for what seemed like five minutes. I was incredibly excited when I got to Houston and I loved every press conference we'd ever had. But I'm so grateful I wasn't at that press conference in February, where I know two of my friends were truly struggling.

They finally got through the press conference, and Van and Kim went to his office and talked and cried. It felt good for Van to sit there with Kim for a moment and tell her how he really felt. Van said that it probably wasn't fair, because when they where done he felt a lot better but he knew what kind of fight she still had in front of her. He knew it would take a lot of effort before Kim felt any better.

Shortly thereafter, Kim had surgery to remove the cancer in her brain. It was the first step in a very long process. Every time Van told someone that Kim was scheduled to have brain surgery, he couldn't believe the words were actually coming out of his mouth. Kim Perrot, the point guard who'd helped him win so many games in Houston, so full of life and energy, was now going into brain surgery. He had a hard time with it.

Van was at the hospital when Kim's surgery was completed. When she could see her first visitors, Kim's mother, Connie, asked Van to come into the room with her and Cynthia. Although Van couldn't wait to see Kim, he didn't feel like it was his place to be one of her first visitors, but Connie insisted that he visit with them, so he made those tough steps into Kim's room.

When they finally caught a glimpse of Kim, she met their eyes and forced a grin. She said, "Hi mom. Hi Cynthia. Coach, you better not find yourself a new point guard; I'm gonna be your girl."

Van was a little hesitant in taking the Houston job because he didn't see a good post player and he didn't see a point guard on the team's early roster. There were some great players assembled, but he knew without a point guard, they didn't have a shot at winning a championship. They didn't draft a point guard that first season and he hoped to get lucky in the free-agency camp. He got lucky and was blessed to have found Kim Perrot.

"If I hadn't taken the job because I was scared I wouldn't find a point guard, I would have never had the chance to get to know her," he said. "She was a fighter and fought the cancer that ravaged her body as best she could, and I think she knew she always had me in her corner willing to fight right alongside her."

Monica Lamb, the starting center during the second championship season, put it best when she said: "This disease chose the wrong person to pick a fight with." Unfortunately, Kim lost the fight, but it's hard to believe how the city of Houston got behind her and her battle with cancer. Kim's will to live will forever inspire the citizens of Houston, and that will forever prove that cancer did indeed choose the wrong person to pick a fight with.

Van didn't give Kim Perrot much of a chance to make Houston's team back in 1997. He knows now that without her his team would have had a much tougher time winning championships in 1997, 1998 and—even though she never played a second—in 1999. From the time training camp opened in April 1999 to the final buzzer in the WNBA championship in September 1999, that team was playing for Kim Perrot.

Following the 1998 championship the team finally got it right and had bottles of champagne in the locker room for a celebration. I walked into the locker room with Van after a couple of interviews, and Kim was waiting for him as we made our turn into the room. She sprayed a direct hit on Van with an entire bottle of the stuff. Van and many other players on the team retaliated by showering her with bottle after bottle of champagne. She didn't mind, didn't run away, didn't fight it at all and screamed, "I feel like Mike, baby. Keep it comin', I feel like Mike!"

Little did any of us know at that time that she was not only celebrating a WNBA championship, but also the last basketball game she would ever play. After the Comets won the 1999 championship and the 16,285 fans were screaming "Number 3 for Number 10", Megan Bonifas gave Kim's jersey to Cynthia Cooper for the trophy presentation. It was an amazing scene when Cynthia ran around the court with Kim's jersey in her hand, and everyone there knew that Kim was among them that day. There wasn't a dry eye in the place; the crowd noise was thunderous amidst a mixture of cheers and tears. The video board in Compaq Center showed a headshot of Kim, and everyone had to look *up* to see her. It really felt like she was there that day.

If even one other person would have agreed with me in April of 1997 to cut her from the free-agency camp, no one would have had the chance to get to know her and see her showcase her incredible skills. Now, when I think about my three years in Houston, I can't help but think of her contributions, her hustle, her inspiration, and I know her laugh will forever echo in my head.

Chapter 12
A Dynasty is Made

THE COMETS PREPARED FOR the 1999 season with Kim on their minds but not on their court. Although the team doctor's diagnosis was grim, Van still held out hope that she might return and play before the season was out. It was probably wishful thinking more than anything else because he knew there were a lot of things she could do on the court, and he would really miss her friendship when the team was on the road.

Fortunately for Houston, the core from the 1998 championship team returned: four starters, Cynthia Cooper, Sheryl Swoopes, Tina Thompson, and Monica Lamb were all ready to defend the title. Polina Tzekova, the team's number one pick in the 1998 draft, was also in Houston for the upcoming season, and she ended up playing most of the minutes at center. But a huge question mark remained at point guard. Cooper could run the point in a pinch but it wasn't the strongest part of her game. Janeth Arcain played point guard in spots, but she wasn't Van's answer to play point guard fulltime.

Kim's illness had already affected the team, and the season was still months out. The WNBA draft now became a critical issue for Van and his coaching staff because they had such a huge hole to fill where Kim once played. However, Van picked up two point guards in the 1999 draft when they selected Sonja Henning in the second round (24th overall) and Jennifer Rizzotti in the fourth round (48th overall).

Initially, Van had hoped to draft a point guard in the first round, but later decided to select the best player available at number twelve. Natalia Zasulskaya, of Russia, was still around at number twelve, and Van selected her hoping there would still be a point guard left in the second round. But two point guards went early in that round as Kedra Holland-Corn went to Sacramento with the fourteenth pick and Debbie Black went to Utah with the fifteenth. Van knew Holland-Corn, Black or Sonja Henning would be available at number twenty-four, and he got his point guard.

Henning got the nod to start at point guard when the team opened the season on June 10 in Orlando. The familiar face of Kim Perrot would not be there to lead the Comets in 1999, and Henning had a tough task of winning over her new coach, her new teammates, and the entire city of Houston. But she filled in nicely for Perrot and guided the Comets to the best record in the league, at 26-6.

"I'm not here to take Kim's place," Sonja told the *Houston Chronicle*. She came into a difficult situation and played under a lot of pressure with the Kim situation looming over the team's every move. She came from a very structured college program at Stanford and had to adapt to Van's loosely run practices and shoot-arounds.

She caught Van's eye in training camp when she and Jennifer Rizzoti were battling for the starting point guard position. She never backed down from guarding Cynthia Cooper, which impressed Van throughout the entire camp. But what put her over the edge was when Van split up the team one practice and Sonja was put on the 'white,' or reserve team. The starters always wear red in Van's practices. Ninety-nine times out of a hundred, the red team defeats the white team in five-on-five drills, but Sonja willed the whites to

victory and hit some big shots over Cynthia, Sheryl
Swoopes, and Tina Thompson.

"There's just something special about her," Van told Kevin
Cook after that practice. "There's something about her that's
going to carry us through."

Henning's contributions were overlooked by many in
the league, but at the end of the season Mary Murphy, of
Lifetime Television, recognized her. Murphy's season-ending "Murph Awards" recognized Sonja as one of the more
under-appreciated players in the WNBA after she showed
the ability to keep Houston together while they were going through such a tough time. It was an admirable dis-
tinction handed down by *Lifetime*, but it was their predictions earlier in the year that upset Van and the rest of the
Comets.

In its opening broadcast of the season, *Lifetime* made
predictions for the 1999 WNBA season, including who
they thought would win the championship. Fran Harris
picked Phoenix, and Murphy picked Los Angeles. Phoenix
didn't qualify for the post-season, and Houston eliminated
Los Angeles in the Western Conference Finals. After the
regular season was over, the *Lifetime* broadcasters still didn't
pick Houston to repeat during their playoff preview show:
Murphy thought Sacramento would win the championship, and Reggie Miller picked Los Angeles.

"I couldn't believe *Lifetime* didn't pick us to win it," Van
said. "We went 27-3 the previous year and had almost everybody back except Kim. I think everyone knew we wouldn't
be 27-3 again, but we didn't even get a sniff from them and
their predictions."

What made the selections even worse was what *Lifetime*
did before Houston defeated New York in game one of the
WNBA Finals at Madison Square Garden. They were now
confident in the Comets and it was a unanimous choice
among the broadcasters that Houston would now win in

two games. Predictions get a lot easier when there're only two teams remaining.

Although Van continued to point out *Lifetime's* predictions throughout the season, he and the network had fun with it too. After a Comets playoff win televised by *Lifetime*, Van joined the broadcast team courtside, grabbed a headset, and thanked them for their predictions on the playoff preview show. "Y'all have inspired us throughout the playoffs," Van said on the air.

❖

Houston opened the season with seven straight wins, tying a WNBA record for wins to start a season. New York also did it in 1997, but it was quite obvious from the opening tip that Houston had all intentions of defending their title. They lost to the expansion Orlando Miracle at home to snap their seven-game win streak, but the Comets responded with four in a row and were off to an 11-1 start. The rest of the league shook their collective heads and wondered how any one was going to stop the Comets.

It looked like the rest of the teams would get help: Houston's center, Monica Lamb, suffered a freak season-ending injury midway through the year at a shoot-around session one morning before a game. Houston has an unusually aggressive shoot-around session on game days. Most teams run through their offense and, well, shoot around at morning shoot-arounds. But the Comets always went full throttle, five-on-five every time they got together, shoot-around or not.

Tammy Jackson threw in an entry pass to Monica and the ball was deflected. As Sheryl Swoopes was reaching for a ball, her finger caught Monica's eye; instantly the Comets' inside game took a jolt. Monica lay on the ground for a moment and no one thought it was a serious injury until she rolled over and the Compaq Center floor was a pool of blood. Monica drenched two towels with blood; she was carted away in an ambulance and stayed in the hospital for over a week, trying to regain sight in the eye.

Van gets queasy at the sight of blood and he immediately turned away. Tammy Jackson pulled the team together and they said a prayer for Monica on the team's bench. Van stopped practice and the team said one more prayer at mid-court before leaving the arena. It seemed this up-and-down season of emotions would never stop, but Van and the Comets were actually just getting started with the emotional roller-coaster ride the third season would present.

After that injury, Van told me that he thought his team was snake-bit and couldn't catch a break. I reminded him that just then he was the two-time WNBA Coach of the Year, his team had won back-to-back championships, won 90 percent of their games the year before, and looked to shatter that record with their current pace. Injuries slowed them down, but Van reloaded and the Comets cruised to the post-season.

At the midway point the season was already a grind for Van, so the first-ever WNBA All-Star Game was a great release. Van looked forward to the All-Star Game as much as any other game he'd coached in the league's short history, because he knew they were making history again.

The Comets had three players represented, in Sheryl Swoopes, Cynthia Cooper and Tina Thompson. The game was played in New York, one of Van's favorite cities, and he brought his entire family to the WNBA's midseason event. It was a great experience for Van on the court, but he also felt satisfied knowing he was able to provide this opportunity to his entire family.

He had some reservations about coaching eleven of the greatest players in the game because he knew they were all superstars and knew they all wanted to shine in the first All-Star Game. But after the team's first practice, it came together; the entire group loosened up and made life easier on Van. He told Yolanda Griffith, the league's eventual

MVP in her third season out of Sacramento, that he couldn't decide whom to start at center between she and Jennifer Gillom.

"Yolanda, I hate to do this to you because I know you're having a great year, but I think I'm going to start Jennifer Gillom because I wouldn't be here and would have never gotten the Houston job if it weren't for her," he told her.

"That's fine with me. Besides, you're the coach," Griffith said. Van couldn't have asked for a better bunch of All-Stars than the eleven he got in the 1999 game in New York.

This was the league's premier event and a lot of celebrities were at the game and the festivities surrounding the weekend. He'd met Tyra Banks and Spike Lee before, but there were a lot of new celebrities coming out for the All-Star Game.

"Dad, I can't believe an ol' country boy from Louisville, Mississippi is hobnobbing with these famous folks," Renee told him at a dinner at the Hard Rock Café in Manhattan.

"Like who?" Van asked as he scanned the room.

"Well, right over there is Joan Jett," Renee said as she pointed across the room. "And sitting right over there is Queen Latifah."

"I don't have a clue who you're talking about," he said. "Unless they were in a John Wayne movie, they're not going to mean a thing to me."

But Van could tell that his kids were impressed that these famous people were coming up to him. Later in the evening, Van bought a Hard Rock Café tee shirt and walked up to Queen Latifah.

"Hey Queeny, could you sign this tee shirt for my grandbaby?"

❖

After starting 11-1, Houston went 14-4 over their next eighteen games before Kim died. On Sunday, August 15, she was flown back to Houston from Tijuana, Mexico, where she was receiving alternative treatment for the cancer. Van and Cynthia were at the airport when the Life Flight landed. Cynthia approached Kim when they got her on the ground, but it hurt Van too much to see his point guard, no, his friend, in such pain. He could hear her moan in pain when they lifted her from the helicopter to the waiting gurney.

On Monday, August 16, just three days before Kim passed, Cynthia visited her in the hospital, left for a game against Utah at Compaq Center, scored a WNBA season-high forty-two points, and immediately returned to the hospital to be with Kim. When she died on August 19, the Comets were 25-5 and rolling through the regular season. For thirty straight games they played with Kim Perrot on their minds. Throughout the season Kim was at many of Houston's games. The night she received her 1998 championship ring was an emotional one, and there were also games when Kim sat on the bench as a cheerleader. Her uniform stayed in her locker the entire season and the Comets couldn't go very far without a reminder of Number 10.

Van was named the WNBA Coach of the Year in 1997 and 1998. But he feels that if he deserved the award in any year it would be for his efforts in 1999. Ironically, the 1999 vote was the closest of the three.

"I was happy to win the award the first two years, but I feel like I really earned it the third year," he said. "We had so much going on, on and off the court, and I think I had to use my coaching abilities to the fullest the third season. We didn't do a lot of things differently on the court than in previous years, but it took all I had to keep this group of ten players together during an extremely fragile four-month period."

The Comets thought about canceling their game in Los Angeles on August 20; just one day after Kim died. They had two games remaining on their schedule, and Van talked to the team about postponing the game. He asked them, but he knew—he knew Kim would have been kicking them in the butt if they hadn't played. The game wasn't canceled and Van led his troops into battle at the Great Western Forum just one day after Kim died.

Cynthia Cooper made the trip to Los Angeles and arriving at the Forum just hours before tip-off. She spent the night before in Houston, sitting beside her friend, comforting her as she slowly slipped from this life. But Cynthia didn't leave her team, and made it to Los Angeles—as a spectator. It was the first time in franchise history that Number 14 would not compete for the Comets and the first time Van would coach this team without the two-time MVP on the court.

Following Kim's death, the WNBA produced a thirty-second tribute video that they wanted shown before player introductions in all WNBA cities. It was a gripping thirty seconds, the kind that make you appreciate every moment you spent with Kim. Van knew it would be too much for his team to handle just before tip-off against Los Angeles, so the Sparks waited until halftime to show the tape.

As Van and his team took the floor that night, you could see there wasn't an ounce of zip in any of them. They were completely drained of emotion and the last thing on their minds was a basketball game. As the national anthem played before the start of the game, Cynthia Cooper sobbed on the court and Tina Thompson and Sheryl Swoopes weren't far behind. I watched Van during the anthem as he fought back tears as best he could. He had a tight lip and a clenched jaw during the entire rendition, but he made it through.

Although it was an extremely sad night for everyone in the place, this was a huge game for the Sparks as they were still battling for playoff position. A win would secure them home-court in the first round of the playoffs against Sacramento. The Comets were down, but just like any competitor, the Sparks couldn't—and didn't—ease up. They were there to do one thing: win.

Houston took the floor with only two of the original five starters from last year's 1998-championship team: Sheryl Swoopes and Tina Thompson started the game against Los Angeles. It looked strange from the sidelines to see such a different Houston lineup starting a game. The Comets lost the game 68-64 and emotions were running high in the Forum. It was a huge win for the Sparks.

Although the game meant absolutely nothing to Houston, because they'd secured the number one seed in the playoffs several days earlier, you would have never guessed it by Van's reaction during and following the game. As the teams battled back-and-forth in the final ten minutes, a questionable call happened directly in front of the Houston bench. The call didn't go Houston's way and Van blew up on the sidelines more than I'd ever seen him before. I've seen him scream and yell and rip off his jacket, but never on the sidelines. You could see the emotions beginning to overcome him and he was whistled for a technical foul. Moments later, after taking off his jacket and throwing it to the bench, he was given his second technical—an automatic ejection.

The Forum was going nuts. There's nothing better than seeing the opposing coach losing his or her composure, and Van was melting down in front of everyone in the building. After his ejection, Tina Thompson walked up to the official who gave Van the boot and said, "We've had kind of a tough weekend. Do you think you might cut us a break?" Fortunately for Van, Tina's talking saved him an ejection and a sizeable fine. Fortunately for the WNBA, Tina's talking saved them an incredible amount of embarrassment. For as much publicity as the Kim Perrot and Houston Comets story had generated, the last thing the league needed was publicity about the team's head coach being ejected just one day after Kim's death.

But if anyone thought the meltdown on the court was

bad, they were in for a shock as Van and the Comets left the floor after losing to Los Angeles. As Van and his coaching staff were heading to the tunnel back to the locker rooms, a Sparks fan said, "C'mon Van. Don't be such a big baby— quit crying." Kevin Cook heard the fan and began scaling the stands, looking to get at this guy.

"I'm gonna kick your ass," Kevin screamed to the rambunctious crowd, doing everything he could to get over the guardrail that separated him from them. "Yeah, me too," Van said in a less intimidating manner but with fire in his eyes. Somehow Van doesn't strike the fear of God into people when he's ready to fight, but he meant it that night in Los Angeles.

It took two security guards, a Sparks coach, and an act of God to get Kevin down from the stands. He was ready to take on anyone who was willing to fight, and he came completely unglued in the midst of all the chaos. They finally got him down and back to the locker room, where I met him. I hadn't seen the confrontation, so I didn't know Kevin's state at the time. I tried making small talk with him about the game and I could tell by the look in his eyes that something had gone down just moments before.

"I'm an exposed nerve, Tom. An exposed nerve," he said.

Okay. It was obvious this team had had enough and all the emotions of an incredible year were finally catching up with them. They couldn't fight back the feelings any longer and everyone reacted differently. Van was extremely angry after the game, and that confrontation in the stands didn't help.

"If I don't have a heart attack tonight, Tom, I've never going to have one," Van said in a small VIP room outside the team's dressing room. The mood finally began to lighten about a half-hour after the game, and we started to laugh at Kevin's Mike Tyson imitation in the stands.

"I wonder how you and I would have looked in orange, Cooker," Van said to Kevin as they laughed. "We almost spent the night in the Los Angeles County jail!" The team needed a laugh because tough times and a lot of tears were ahead.

The following day, Saturday, August 21, the team traveled to Sacramento and finished out the regular season with a win. On Sunday, August 22, the team traveled back to Houston and prepared for one of the toughest weeks of their lives. On Monday, August 23, the Comets organization held a "Celebration of Life" memorial for Kim at Second Baptist Church, in Houston. There were many speakers that day, but Van and Cynthia stood out. Where they found the strength to get up and speak is beyond any sense of reality for me.

Van got to the podium visibly shaken, with his voice cracking, "In the spring of 1997, Les Alexander hired me to coach the Comets." He had to stop for a moment and fight off the tears that were building in his heartbroken body. He put his left hand to his face and started to cry but regained his composure when the audience applauded. He looked down and saw Cynthia and Tina smiling back at him and it gave him strength to carry on.

He told several stories about how the two had become friends over the past two years and about how he didn't like her as a player when he first met her. You hoped he could get through it, because everybody in the place and those watching on TV knew he was hurting. He did battle through it and here's how he finished:

"What a fun person. What a great time she had and she had a great joy for life. There will never be another Kim Perrot in my mind—just never will be. I want to leave you with this: You know, I thought about God kind of holding her hand through this illness, and when he came, he kindly put her in his arms and here's what he said: 'Well-done, my good and faithful servant.' "

What an emotional time it was for Van and the Comets. All this was going on and his team should have been gearing up for a third championship run, but during that time no one cared about a championship, a basketball game, or anything else except Kim Perrot.

On Tuesday, August 24, the team traveled to Lafayette, Louisiana for Kim's funeral, and on Wednesday, August 25, they traveled back to Los Angeles for game one of the Western Conference Finals against the Sparks. In six days Van and his team had lost their inspirational leader to cancer, lost an emotional game to the Sparks, traveled to Sacramento, traveled to Houston, sat through a gut-wrenching memorial service in Houston, traveled to Lafayette for Kim's funeral, traveled back to Houston and then on to Los Angeles. Not the easiest way to prepare for a playoff run.

❖

It was no surprise that Houston came out flat against Los Angeles in game one of the playoffs. They looked like a team that had just gone through an unimaginable week—they had.   The Sparks took a four-point lead into halftime and built it to as many as seventeen in the second half before winning 75-60. The Comets didn't have a chance in that game. As I sat there and watched, I continued to imagine Kim in the huddle when they were down. "We can do this. C'mon ladies, we gotta fight! You gotta want it!"

After the game I talked with Van and he wasn't as down as I thought he would be. Again, he knew he had the better team and he was confident they would come back strong in game two back in Houston.

"When I look at it now, I realize we had absolutely no chance of winning that game" Van said. "I just can't believe everything we've been through. It's been a whirlwind for the last two weeks and we just can't get going. We gotta start playing again. Kim wouldn't appreciate this effort at all."

Houston did respond in game two, drilling Los Angeles 83-55 at Compaq Center. The Sparks entered the game quite confident after beating the Comets at the Great Western Forum and realized they were just one win away from advancing to the WNBA Finals. But entering the game, Houston was 4-0 in post-season elimination games and their drubbing of the Sparks made it 5-0.

Game three was different. The Sparks didn't back down from Houston, and led by as many as nine in the first half. They led by as many as three with eight minutes to play, but Houston outscored the Sparks 18-7 over the final eight minutes to win the series. Van and his staff made a bold move with 8:21 to play, when Tina Thompson picked up her fifth foul. He immediately turned to his bench and asked his coaches, "Take her out or let it roll?" Everyone on the bench wanted to leave her in and Tina played the rest of the way with five fouls.

It was a move that could have cost him the game because Los Angeles is so much bigger than the Comets. If Tina had fouled out, Van would have been blamed for an inevitable loss. He rolled the dice and it worked, and no one in the media ever picked up on it or ever asked him about it. But that's the nature of coaching: blamed if you lose, and great players if you win.

In another three-game series in the Eastern Conference, the New York Liberty defeated the Charlotte Sting for the right to play the Comets in the WNBA Championship. It was a rematch of the inaugural season championship game, only this time it was a three-game series. Van felt like game two and three against Los Angeles had gotten his team back into playing form and he was comfortable with their chances against New York.

Van loves playing in New York. He's often asked how much he hates it there because of the way New York fans get on him and his players, but he actually likes it. It's one of his favorite WNBA cities to visit. After all, he's got connections with the seat holders behind home plate at Yankee Stadium.

Houston went to Madison Square Garden and drilled the Liberty 73-60 for a game one victory. With two games at home at Compaq Center, a third WNBA championship seemed inevitable. Including the regular season and playoffs, the Comets were 35-2 at Compaq Center in 1998 and 1999, and the thought of the less talented New York Liberty winning two in Houston seemed improbable.

I traveled to Houston for the Finals against New York and got to the arena early for game two. I wanted to see a lot of old friends and co-workers, but as soon as Van got to Compaq Center he found me. "Boy, I'm really nervous today," he said, a hundred miles an hour. "Come with me, I gotta walk and talk to somebody."

We went back to his office about two hours before tip-off and talked for a long time. "I'm just so full of emotions right now," he said. "I don't know what's wrong with me. I feel like I'm going to cry."

"Going to cry, why?" I asked. "I don't know," he replied. "I guess I've been thinking about Kim, about how I don't want to let my team down. I really feel a lot of pressure to win this thing for her. I just can't believe the way this city has gotten behind her and how big this game has become. Can you believe it?"

"It is pretty amazing," I said, "but I wouldn't worry. I mean, c'mon—you really think New York can come into this place and win back-to-back games?"

"You're probably right, but I just feel a little funny. I don't want to let my team or this organization down," he said. "I just got a funny feeling something strange is going to happen today."

❖

Van finally got his nerves settled as it got closer to game time. He's always been like that: he gets really nervous hours before tip-off, but calms down as the time draws near. He took time out to take a photo with his entire family for NBA Entertainment. Before the family joined him, he took a photograph with his pride and joy—one in each arm: his grandson Nicholas on one side and newly born grandson Jacob on the other. Jacob Winston Chancellor was born to Angela and Johnny prior to the start of the third season. When Johnny was growing up, Van called him 'Big Jake,' in honor of Van's favorite actor, John Wayne. Johnny always told Van that if he ever had a son, he was going to name him Jacob so the name "Jake" would continue on. Van's proper name is Winston Van Chancellor, and Van's father is also Winston, hence Jacob's middle name.

The photo calmed him down because he was with two guys who didn't care if he won, lost, or tied, they were just glad to be around him. But after the photo he immediately headed to the locker room and got into his game mode. He was walking a mile a minute and was clinching his hands, all the while talking to anyone who would listen. He had a few final thoughts for his coaches before he left the room.

"Megan, you got my candy?" he asked Megan Bonifas, the new PR director for the team. Ah, the old times. There were several nights when I was still with the Comets that I questioned my four years of college because I spent half the night running down his candy. I'm sure she felt the same way.

Van had his team fired up for game two with New York, as they were only forty minutes away from a "three-peat." It was obvious to all 16,285 fans in Compaq Center that this team was playing for Kim Perrot. Heck, the crowd was cheering for Kim Perrot and "Number 3 for Number 10" signs could be seen all over the arena. Signs, buttons, stickers and banners were everywhere; Houston was primed for a big-time celebration after its Comets dusted off New York.

Houston built a 15-2 lead to open the game and it seemed now just a formality before the champagne was uncorked and the Comets' locker room turned into the most popular dance club in the city. I was sitting with CNNSI's Tom Rinaldi, who was covering his first WNBA game. He leaned over to me at that point and asked, "Is it over?" I nodded with confidence and told him he could start working on his story. The Comets increased their lead to as many as eighteen when Tina Thompson's free throw made it 37-19 with 1:44 to play in the first half. The Comets were running away with it and took a 37-23 lead into halftime. That's when they stopped playing.

Van was comfortable with his lead and didn't give a blistering halftime speech. He was easy on them because, frankly, he thought his players' emotions had been through too much, and he was happy with the way they were playing and with the comfortable lead. He was very business-like during his halftime talk and stirred as little emotion as he could. But in the New York locker room, Liberty head coach Richie Adubato must have been giving the halftime speech of a lifetime, and Crystal Robinson must have been listening.

Robinson had just three points at the break on 1-of-6 shooting. She finished with a game-high twenty-one points, went 5-for-5 from the field in the second half and finished with four three-pointers. New York slowly climbed back into it and Van knew he had been too easy on his team at halftime.

"I was afraid something like that was going to happen," he said. "We were in there celebrating at halftime because we all thought we had the thing won. We were notorious for that all season. We would get a comfortable lead, get lazy, start playing one-on-one basketball and blow the lead. I told them a hundred times throughout the year that if we keep doing that, sometime it's going to catch up to us on a freak shot at the buzzer. I told them that all the time."

New York didn't waste any time cutting into the four-teen-point halftime bulge and cut the gap to two with 15:22 to play when Robinson hit a three-pointer to make it 39-37. The Liberty had put together a scoring spurt of their own and it was an entirely new game. Houston was able to hold off New York for a little while longer, but Robinson's three-pointer with 11:55 to play gave the Liberty their first lead of the game at 42-40.

Van used a timeout to stop New York's momentum. "La-dies, we have just simply stopped playing defense," he said. "We're just kiddin' ourselves out here if we don't start play-ing some defense."

The timeout seemed to help and the Comets went on a 12-1 run to open the lead back to nine at 52-43. But this was do-or-die time for New York, and the Liberty kept coming and scored the next nine points to tie the game at 52 with 6:30 remaining. The teams exchanged leads several times over the next six minutes and 28.6 seconds. It looked like Houston had finally stopped the seesaw battle when Tina Thompson's turn-around jumper with 2.4 seconds re-maining gave the Comets a 67-65 lead.

The Compaq Center erupted and the scene was quite familiar—it looked like history repeating itself. There was confusion under the basket after Thompson scored. There were still 2.4 seconds remaining and New York's Teresa Weatherspoon was waiting for the inbounds pass. Van was frantic on the sidelines, pleading, begging for his team to put token pressure on Weatherspoon as she brought the ball up the floor. Only Tina Thompson saw him, and she overran the play.

Cynthia Cooper, Sheryl Swoopes and everyone else with a white uniform that day had dropped back into their standard half-court defense to defend against any three-pointers. But while they were dropping back, Weatherspoon's fifty-footer was in flight as the buzzer sounded. The confetti began to fall, the crowd was out of control and Tina Turner's *Simply the Best* began to get louder as the celebration began at Compaq Center. But while all this was going on, Weatherspoon's shot was sailing through the air, on course for a direct hit. She hit it at the buzzer and Houston's emotionally filled, up-and-down season just would not end.

"When she let that baby go, I said to myself, 'Well I better get our team up for tomorrow,'" Van said. "That thing looked dead-on. People don't believe me that I said that to myself, but I did. I knew the second she let it fly that it was going in—no doubt."

❖

Take every heart-wrenching loss Van's ever had to go through, wrap them all up into one, and they don't come close to how it felt when Weatherspoon's prayer was answered from fifty feet out. He was right though; something strange was going to happen.

He was in no mood to speak after the game. He did his mandatory press conference, grabbed his jacket from the locker room and left the building. He and Betty went straight home, where he watched the game over and over, trying to figure out what went wrong in the second half. Although Weatherspoon's shot was the game-winner, Van knew his team had lost the game way before she ever attempted the shot and he knew it should have never come to that. There was a breakdown on defense and his team just simply quit playing.

Van was sick the evening of Saturday, September 4 after Weatherspoon's shot banked in. He had a hard time sleeping as the night wore on, and he asked Betty for some aspirin to fight off a pounding headache and nagging stomachache. Betty knew best and tricked him by giving him two tablets of Tylenol PM to make him drowsy. It worked;

he finally let the game fade and he finally slept for part of the night.

"I asked Betty for some aspirin, but she could have given me anything because I was so miserable," he said. "I was at an all-time low and I just took whatever she gave me. Betty said I was lower than a flea's belly, so she took matters into her own hands to help me sleep to get the game off my mind."

But Van woke up in the middle of the night and began to feel a little better about things. He calmed himself when he thought about the fight in his team, and had a feeling they wouldn't let something like blowing a huge lead happen two days in a row at Compaq Center. Indeed, Van was feeling better but he was in no shape to lead a 'self-help' group. For the first time in twelve hours he didn't feel like jumping off the nearest bridge—at that point, a huge step.

He fell back asleep for a few hours and when he woke up on Sunday morning he headed to church. "I did the best I could at church that day, but I could only get to adult Sunday school," he said. "I just don't think I could have stayed still sittin' through an entire sermon."

He arrived at Compaq Center not excited, not nervous, and not emotional, just drained. He was pale and you could sense he just wanted the season to end—with a win. I walked to his office at about the same time I had the day before to see how he was doing. His mood had changed dramatically in a twenty-four-hour span. When I walked in he was sleeping on his couch and Johnny was in the room with him. He looked up for a moment, quietly said, "Hey Tom," and promptly rolled over with his back to me. I didn't need another hint—I was gone.

Van got his team together in the locker room before tip-off, and scribbled five keys to winning on the chalkboard at the front of the room. You've got to be watching and listening to Van when he's writing things down on a board for his team. When he's in front of his team before a game, or even a practice, he's flying, and if you're not there to see and hear what he's writing, it's tough to read a word. His five keys to the Comets on September 5, 1999 were:

1) Get a body on somebody and win the battle of the boards.

In game two vs. New York, the Comets were outrebounded 34-28. If there's anything that drives Van crazy on the basketball court it's not getting position for a rebound and losing that battle to the competition. In game three, Houston outrebounded the Liberty 36-28.

2)   Stay out of foul trouble.

Van wanted to keep the Liberty out of the penalty until late in the game. New York was able to get back into Game two by going to the free throw line early in the second half. It helped erase a fourteen-point halftime deficit. In game three the Liberty weren't in the penalty until extremely late in the game, when it was out of reach.

3)   Don't give up the lead.

In game two, the Comets blew an eighteen-point lead and were notorious all season for squandering leads. In game three, Houston led 33-25 at halftime and the Liberty got no closer than seven in the second half, as the Comets increased the lead to as many as eighteen in the second half.

4)   Fight through screens.

Van didn't like the way his team quit playing defense in the second half against New York in game two. One of the reasons Crystal Robinson went 5-for-5 in the second half and finished with a game-high twenty-one points; eighteen of which came in the second half, was because she was so wide open and had good looks at the basket. In game three, the twenty-two second half points and the forty-seven total points put up by New York were both season lows against the Comets in 1999.

5)   Get Cooper in position to make plays.

Van wasn't necessarily looking for more scoring out of Cynthia, although she did tie a season low with twelve points in game two, but he wanted to get her in a better position to make more plays. In game three, she finished with a game-high twenty-four points, went to the line fifteen times, grabbed six rebounds and had three steals.

Those were the keys to victory for Van, and his team responded. They usually did respond when their backs were to the wall, and after New York's miraculous comeback a day earlier, Van had their full attention.

Ironically, just as in 1997 against New York, the veteran Tammy Jackson stepped up and had a huge game on a huge day. She finished with a game-high eleven rebounds and a game-high three blocked shots, and scored seven points— all in twenty-six minutes of play. Jackson has three championship rings with Houston, but it almost ended after just one. Prior to the 1998 season, Van was unable to protect her in the WNBA's expansion draft, and the Washington Mystics selected her. But early in the 1998 season Washington waived her and Van couldn't get on the phone fast enough with the league to re-sign her.

"It's amazing how much Tammy Jackson has contributed in the playoffs for us for three straight years," Van said. "We took her in the second round in the 1997 WNBA draft and we would have never guessed how big an impact she was going to have on this franchise. I'm so grateful that we drafted her and got her back from Washington. It broke my heart when we lost her in the expansion draft, but she was meant to be in Houston. She was meant to be a Comet in the WNBA."

Game three against New York really wasn't much of a game at all. The Comets trailed just once, 11-10 early in the first half. As they increased their lead in the second half, and it was obvious they were going to win their third

WNBA championship in as many years, the Comets bench began to celebrate on a Janeth Arcain basket with just under a minute to play. Houston held a 59-41 lead and the Compaq Center decibel level began to rise for the third straight season.

As the bench began its pre-celebration celebration, Van got on them and told them to sit down and not get excited just yet. But, just as in the first championship when he got mad at Kim Perrot's flashy pass, Van realized later that he'd been wrong and he apologized to the bench in the final moments. They didn't care though—they were too busy celebrating.

When the final buzzer sounded, Van felt an incredible sense of relief. The turbulent and emotional season was finally over and they had won their third championship in as many seasons. The first two titles were great, but this one meant so much more to Van and his players. They played through so much the entire season, and anything short of a championship as they played for Kim Perrot would have been disheartening.

❖

Just prior to the 1998 WNBA Finals, NBC did a story on Van, previewing the upcoming playoffs. They were defending 1997 champions and had just completed a 27-3 season. They were clearly favorites to win their second championship in as many years.

The interviewer asked, "Van, you've got a great team and they look poised to win another championship. Actually, your team looks good enough to win as many WNBA championships as you want. What's your goal for the next five, ten years? Is it to have five to ten championship rings on your finger?"

Van replied with his infectious grin: "I gotta tell ya. I might be the luckiest man alive, and it has nothing to do with basketball. I could have a million rings and I'd trade 'em all in for my family, my grandbaby and the great times that we have. I just hope I'm around in five or ten years so I can continue to enjoy my life with them."

In 1965, Van Chancellor coached his first game at the age of twenty-one and was destroyed by Edinberg High School in central Mississippi. Something tells me his last game will be a win in the WNBA Finals in a season yet to come, because the man begins every season he coaches looking for "Nothin' but a championship."

POST GAME PRESS CONFERENCE
GAME 3, WNBA FINALS, SEPTEMBER 5, 1999

Van's opening remarks: "Today, after yesterday, I tried to cover all of my bases. Number one, after shoot-around, I went to church today. I just wanted the Lord to know whose side I was on just in case he had any interest in the WNBA. Then I got out my lucky coat, tie and pants that I wore in 1997. My clothier, Harold, said, 'Whatever you do, don't wear that. People will think that you're not getting clothes that are new.' But I stayed with the look. Then the best thing that ever happened, my boy came in, he's a high school coach and he said, 'Dad, just relax. You're going crazy. You've got great players, just let them play.'

"I'm happy to be here today as three-time champs of the WNBA. It doesn't get any better than this after yesterday. After what this team has gone through, I don't know of any group of players anywhere at anytime in their lives that deserve a championship any more than they do. If you don't think the spirit of Kim Perrot is alive in the Comets' world right now, you're dead wrong. I thought all along that twelve Comets pulling together would be hard to beat because she's still on this team. Her inspiration, I can't tell you what this team has gone through since we learned that she was diagnosed with cancer. I can't tell you some things that are unbelievable that they have gone through. To go through everything personally that this team has, then to lose yesterday in a heartbreaking game and to come back and win today and give up only 47 points, that might be the best defense I've ever seen a team play."

Q: "It seems that every time after a strong defensive performance, you say that was the best defense you've ever seen. Is that the case after today's game?"

Van: "We outrebounded New York 36-28. We ain't outrebounded a team that much since the Korean conflict.

You have to ask me if that was a great defensive game; we only give up forty-seven points in a championship game? Forty-seven points. Yes! I thought Sheryl Swoopes was outstanding on Crystal Robinson today. I thought Cynthia Cooper was great offensively. I thought Tina Thompson was unbelievable and Tammy Jackson had eleven rebounds!"

Q: "Talk about Tammy Jackson's contributions."

Van: "She went in tonight and had eleven boards, seven points, a veteran player. Houston is always going to keep veteran players. We're not worried about a youth movement. I want to win today. So we keep a veteran player like Tammy Jackson who can get eleven boards and when she messes up you can say, 'Tammy, you know you're not rebounding.' And you look at the stat sheet and she has nine. She doesn't let it bother her, she just plays."

Q: "How do you describe Tina Thompson's role on this team?"

Van: "I don't think she's appreciated throughout the league. She's a player that has to guard the other team's best player. She got six rebounds, thirteen points. She's a warrior night after night. I asked her with nine minutes to go if she needed a break and she said, 'Coach, I don't mean this disrespectful, but you're going to make me fightin' mad if you even think about taking me out of the game.'"